D0175994

in
ONE
ACT

Emergent Literatures

Adrienne KENNEDY

in ONE ACT

University of Minnesota Press
Minneapolis   London

Copyright © 1988 by Adrienne Kennedy.
All rights reserved. No part of this publication may be reproduced, stored in a retrieval system, or transmitted, in any form or by any means, electronic, mechanical, photocopying, recording, or otherwise, without the prior written permission of the publisher.

Published by the University of Minnesota Press
111 Third Avenue South, Suite 290, Minneapolis, MN 55420-2520
Seventh printing, 2011
Printed in the United States of America on acid-free paper
Designed by Craig Carnahan.

Funnyhouse of a Negro, copyright © 1962 by Adrienne Kennedy
The Owl Answers, copyright © 1963 by Adrienne Kennedy
A Lesson in Dead Language, copyright © 1968 Adrienne Kennedy
A Rat's Mass, copyright © 1967 by Adrienne Kennedy
Sun, copyright © 1969 by Adrienne Kennedy
A Movie Star Has to Star in Black and White, copyright © 1976 by Adrienne Kennedy

All inquiries about productions should be made to the author's agent: Bridget Aschenberg, International Creative Management, 40 West 57th St., New York, NY 10019. (212) 556-5600

LIBRARY OF CONGRESS
Library of Congress Cataloging-in-Publication Data

Kennedy, Adrienne.
    [Plays]
    Adrienne Kennedy in one act.
      p. cm. — (Emergent literatures)
    Contents: Funnyhouse of a negro — The owl answers — A lesson in dead language — A rat's mass — Sun — A movie star has to star in black and white — Greek adaptations: Electra; Orestes.
    ISBN 0-8166-1691-4   ISBN 0-8166-1692-2 (pbk.)
    I. Title. II. Series
    PS3561.E4252A6 1988
    812'.54 — dc19   87-36463

The University of Minnesota
is an equal-opportunity
educator and employer

For my sons
Adam and Joe

Ellen Holly and Cynthia Belgrave in the East End Theatre (New York) production of *Funnyhouse of a Negro*, January, 1964. Photograph courtesy of Fredrick Eberstadt.

Contents

Preface

More than anything I remember the days surrounding the writing of each of these plays . . . the places . . . Accra Ghana and Rome for *Funnyhouse of a Negro* . . . the shuttered guest house surrounded by gardens of sweet smelling frangipani shrubs . . . in Rome the sunny roof of the apartment on Via Reno . . . the beginnings of *The Owl Answers,* also in Ghana . . . the lines of the play growing on trips to the North as I sought refuge from the heat at the desks of guest houses . . . our wonderful brand new apartment in New York in the Park West Village for *A Rat's Mass* and the enchanting Primrose Hill in London for *Sun* (sitting in the dining room overlooking Chalcot Crescent). Hadn't Sylvia Plath lived across the way in Chalcot Square? And again the Upper West Side of Manhattan for *A Movie Star Has to Star in Black and White* and *Electra* and *Orestes.*

Without exception the days when I am writing are days of images fiercely pounding in my head and days of walking . . . in Ghana, across the campus of Legon . . . in Rome through the Forum, in New York along Columbus Avenue and in London, Primrose Hill (hadn't Karl Marx walked there?) walks and coffee . . . all which seem to put me under a spell of sorts . . . . I am at the typewriter almost every waking moment and suddenly there is a play. It would be impossible to say I wrote them. Somehow under this spell they become written.

A. K.
New York City
Upper West Side, 1987

Acknowledgments

For encouragement and support I really want to thank Michael Kahn, Edward Albee, Ellen Stewart, Mr. and Mrs. Fredrick Eberstadt, Joseph Papp, Robert Brustein, Julia Miles, Wynn Handman, Werner Sollors, Ted Mann, Joseph Chaikin, William Gaskill, Gaby Rodgers, Howard Klein, The Rockefeller Foundation, the Guggenheim Foundation, and Julliard. I also want to acknowledge the work in these plays of so many brilliant and dedicated actors, among them being: Billie Allen, Ellen Holly, Joan Harris, Gilbert Price, Mary Alice, Robbie McCauley, Roger Robinson, Moses Gunn, Cynthia Belgrave, Leonard Frey, and Yaphet Kotto.

And I'd especially like to thank my editors Terry Cochran and Craig Carnahan for their tremendous enthusiasm for putting these plays in one volume.

A. K.

FUNNYHOUSE
of a
NEGRO

Characters

NEGRO-SARAH	
DUCHESS OF HAPSBURG	One of herselves
QUEEN VICTORIA REGINA	One of herselves
JESUS	One of herselves
PATRICE LUMUMBA	One of herselves
SARAH'S LANDLADY	Funnyhouse Lady
RAYMOND	Funnyhouse Man
THE MOTHER	

Author's Note

FUNNYHOUSE of a NEGRO is perhaps clearest and most explicit when the play is placed in the girl Sarah's room. The center of the stage works well as her room, allowing the rest of the stage as the place for herselves. Her room should have a bed, a writing table and a mirror. Near her bed is the statue of Queen Victoria; other objects might

Obie award-winning original production by Barr-Albee-Wilder, at the East End Theater, 1964, directed by Michael Kahn.

be her photographs and her books. When she is placed in her room with her belongings, then the director is free to let the rest of the play happen around her.

BEGINNING: *Before the closed Curtain* A WOMAN *dressed in a white nightgown walks across the Stage carrying before her a bald head. She moves as one in a trance and is mumbling something inaudible to herself. Her hair is wild, straight and black and falls to her waist. As she moves, she gives the effect of one in a dream. She crosses the Stage from Right to Left. Before she has barely vanished, the CURTAIN opens. It is a white satin Curtain of a cheap material and a ghastly white, a material that brings to mind the interior of a cheap casket, parts of it are frayed and look as if it has been gnawed by rats.*

SCENE: TWO WOMEN *are sitting in what appears to be a Queen's chamber. It is set in the middle of the Stage in a strong white LIGHT, while the rest of the Stage is in unnatural BLACKNESS. The quality of the white light is unreal and ugly. The Queen's chamber consists of a dark monumental bed resembling an ebony tomb, a low, dark chandelier with candles, and wine-colored walls. Flying about are great black* RAVENS. QUEEN VICTORIA *is standing before her bed holding a small mirror in her hand. On the white pillow of her bed is a dark, indistinguishable object.* THE DUCHESS OF HAPSBURG *is standing at the foot of the bed. Her back is to us as is the* QUEEN'S. *Throughout the entire scene, they do not move.* BOTH WOMEN *are dressed in royal gowns of white, a white similar to the white of the Curtain, the material cheap satin. Their headpieces are white and of a net that falls over their faces. From beneath both their headpieces springs a headful of wild kinky hair. Although in this scene we do not see their faces, I will describe them now. They look exactly alike and will wear masks or be made up to appear a whitish yellow. It is an alabaster face, the skin drawn tightly over the high cheekbones, great dark eyes that seem gouged out of the head, a high forehead, a full red mouth and a head of frizzy hair. If the characters do not wear a mask then the face must be highly powdered and possess a hard expressionless quality and a stillness as in the face of death. We hear KNOCKING.*

VICTORIA. *(Listening to the knocking.)* It is my father. He is arriving again for the night. *(The* DUCHESS *makes no reply.)* He comes through the jungle to find me. He never tires of his journey.

DUCHESS. How dare he enter the castle, he who is the darkest of them all, the darkest one? My mother looked like a white woman, hair as straight as any white woman's. And at least I am yellow, but he is black, the blackest one of them all. I hoped he was dead. Yet he still comes through the jungle to find me.

(The KNOCKING is louder.)

VICTORIA. He never tires of the journey, does he, Duchess? *(Looking at herself in the mirror.)*

DUCHESS. How dare he enter the castle of Queen Victoria Regina, Monarch of England? It is because of him that my mother died. The wild black beast put his hands on her. She died.

VICTORIA. Why does he keep returning? He keeps

returning forever, coming back ever and keeps coming back forever. He is my father.

DUCHESS. He is a black Negro.

VICTORIA. He is my father. I am tied to the black Negro. He came when I was a child in the south, before I was born he haunted my conception, diseased my birth.

DUCHESS. Killed my mother.

VICTORIA. My mother was the light. She was the lightest one. She looked like a white woman.

DUCHESS. We are tied to him unless, of course, he should die.

VICTORIA. But he is dead.

DUCHESS. And he keeps returning.

(The KNOCKING is louder; BLACKOUT. The LIGHTS go out in the Chamber. Onto the Stage from the Left comes the FIGURE in the white nightgown carrying the bald head. This time we hear her speak.)

MOTHER. Black man, black man, I never should have let a black man put his hands on me. The wild black beast raped me and now my skull is shining. *(She disappears to the Right.)*

(Now the LIGHT is focused on a single white square wall that is to the Left of the Stage, that is suspended and stands alone, of about five feet in dimension and width. It stands with the narrow part facing the audience. A CHARACTER steps through. She is a faceless, dark character with a hangman's rope about her neck and red blood on the part that would be her face. She is the NEGRO. The most noticeable aspect of her looks is her wild kinky hair. It is a ragged head with a patch of hair missing from the

crown which the NEGRO *carries in her hand. She is dressed in black. She steps slowly through the wall, stands still before it and begins her monologue:)*

NEGRO. Part of the time I live with Raymond, part of the time with God, Maxmillian and Albert Saxe Coburg. I live in my room. It is a small room on the top floor of a brownstone in the West Nineties in New York, a room filled with my dark old volumes, a narrow bed and on the wall old photographs of castles and monarchs of England. It is also Victoria's chamber. Queen Victoria Regina's. Partly because it is consumed by a gigantic plaster statue of Queen Victoria who is my idol and partly for other reasons; three steps that I contrived out of boards lead to the statue which I have placed opposite the door as I enter the room. It is a sitting figure, a replica of one in London, and a thing of astonishing whiteness. I found it in a dusty shop on Morningside Heights. Raymond says it is a thing of terror, possessing the quality of nightmares, suggesting large and probable deaths. And of course he is right. When I am the Duchess of Hapsburg I sit opposite Victoria in my head-piece and we talk. The other time I wear the dress of a student, dark clothes and dark stockings. Victoria always wants me to tell her of whiteness. She wants me to tell her of a royal world where everything and everyone is white and there are no unfortunate black ones. For as we of royal blood know, black is evil and has been from the beginning. Even before my mother's hair started to fall out. Before she was raped by a wild black beast. Black was evil.

As for myself I long to become even a more pallid Negro than I am now; pallid like Negroes on the covers of American Negro magazines; soulless, educated and irreligious. I want to possess no moral value, particularly value as to my being. I want not to be. I ask nothing except anonymity. I am an English major, as my mother was when she went to school in Atlanta. My father majored in social work. I am graduated from a city college and have occasional work in libraries, but mostly spend my days preoccupied with the placement and geometric position of words on paper. I write poetry filling white page after white page with imitations of Edith Sitwell. It is my dream to live in rooms with European antiques and my Queen Victoria, photographs of Roman ruins, walls of books, a piano, oriental carpets and to eat my meals on a white glass table. I will visit my friends' apartments which will contain books, photographs of Roman ruins, pianos and oriental carpets. My friends will be white.

I need them as an embankment to keep me from reflecting too much upon the fact that I am a Negro. For, like all educated Negroes—out of life and death essential—I find it necessary to maintain a stark fortress against recognition of myself. My white friends, like myself, will be shrewd, intellectual and anxious for death. Anyone's death. I will mistrust them, as I do myself, waver in their opinion of me, as I waver in the opinion of myself. But if I had not wavered in my opinion of myself, then my hair would never have fallen out. And if my hair hadn't fallen out, I wouldn't have bludgeoned my father's head with an ebony mask.

In appearance I am good-looking in a boring way; no glaring Negroid features, medium nose, medium mouth and pale yellow skin. My one defect is that I have a head of frizzy hair, unmistakably Negro kinky hair; and it is indistinguishable. I would like to lie and say I love Raymond. But I do not. He is a poet and is Jewish. He is very interested in Negroes.

(*The* NEGRO *stands by the wall and throughout her following speech, the following characters come through the wall, disappearing off into varying directions in the darkened night of the Stage:* DUCHESS, QUEEN VICTORIA, JESUS, PATRICE LUMUMBA. JESUS *is a hunchback, yellow-skinned dwarf, dressed in white rags and sandals.* PATRICE LUMUMBA *is a black man. His head appears to be split in two with blood and tissue in eyes. He carries an ebony mask.)*

SARAH (NEGRO). The rooms are my rooms; a Hapsburg chamber, a chamber in a Victorian castle, the hotel where I killed my father, the jungle. These are the places myselves exist in. I know no places. That is, I cannot believe in places. To believe in places is to know hope and to know the emotion of hope is to know beauty. It links us across a horizon and connects us to the world. I find there are no places only my funnyhouse. Streets are rooms, cities are rooms, eternal rooms. I try to create a space for myselves in cities, New York, the midwest, a southern town, but it becomes a lie. I try to give myselves a logical relationship but that too is a lie. For relationships was one of my last religions. I clung loyally to the lie of relationships, again and again seeking to establish a connection between my characters. Jesus is Victoria's son. Mother loved my father before her hair fell out. A loving relationship exists between myself and Queen Victoria, a love between myself and Jesus but they are lies.

(Then to the Right front of the Stage comes the WHITE LIGHT. It goes to a suspended stairway. At the foot of it, stands the LANDLADY. *She is a tall, thin, white woman dressed in a black and red hat and appears to be talking to someone in a suggested open doorway in a corridor of a rooming house. She*

laughs like a mad character in a funnyhouse throughout her speech.)

LANDLADY. *(Who is looking up the stairway.)* Ever since her father hung himself in a Harlem hotel when Patrice Lumumba was murdered she hides herself in her room. Each night she repeats: He keeps returning. How dare he enter the castle walls, he who is the darkest of them all, the darkest one? My mother looked like a white woman, hair as straight as any white woman's. And I am yellow but he, he is black, the blackest one of them all. I hoped he was dead. Yet he still comes through the jungle.

     I tell her: Sarah, honey, the man hung himself. It's not your blame. But, no, she stares at me: No, Mrs. Conrad, he did not hang himself, that is only the way they understand it, they do, but the truth is that I bludgeoned his head with an ebony skull that he carries about with him. Wherever he goes, he carries black masks and heads.

     She's suffering so till her hair has fallen out. But then she did always hide herself in that room with the walls of books and her statue. I always did know she thought she was somebody else, a Queen or something, somebody else.

BLACKOUT

SCENE: *Funnyman's place.*

The next scene is enacted with the DUCHESS *and* RAYMOND. *Raymond's place is suggested as being above the Negro's room and is etched in with a prop of blinds and a bed. Behind the blinds are mirrors and when the blinds are opened and closed by Raymond this is revealed.* RAYMOND *turns out to be the funnyman of the funnyhouse. He is tall, white and ghostly thin and dressed in a black shirt and black trousers in attire suggesting an artist. Throughout his dialogue he laughs. The* DUCHESS *is partially disrobed and it is implied from their attitudes of physical intimacy —he is standing and she is sitting before him clinging to his leg. During the scene* RAYMOND *keeps opening and closing the blinds.*

DUCHESS. *(Carrying a red paper bag.)* My father is arriving and what am I to do?

*(*RAYMOND *walks about the place opening the blinds and laughing.)*

FUNNYMAN. He is arriving from Africa, is he not?
DUCHESS. Yes, yes, he is arriving from Africa.
FUNNYMAN. I always knew your father was African.
DUCHESS. He is an African who lives in the jungle. He is an African who has always lived in the jungle. Yes, he is a nigger who is an African who is a missionary teacher and is now dedicating his life to the erection of a Christian mission in the middle of the jungle. He is a black man.
FUNNYMAN. He is a black man who shot himself when they murdered Patrice Lumumba.
DUCHESS. *(Goes on wildly.)* Yes, my father is a black man who went to Africa years ago as a missionary teacher, got mixed up in politics, was revealed and is now devoting his foolish life to the erection of a Christian mission in the middle of the jungle in one of those newly freed countries. Hide me. *(Clinging to his knees.)* Hide me here so

the nigger will not find me.

FUNNYMAN. *(Laughing.)* Your father is in the jungle dedicating his life to the erection of a Christian mission.

DUCHESS. Hide me here so the jungle will not find me. Hide me.

FUNNYMAN. Isn't it cruel of you?

DUCHESS. Hide me from the jungle.

FUNNYMAN. Isn't it cruel?

DUCHESS. No, no.

FUNNYMAN. Isn't it cruel of you?

DUCHESS. No. *(She screams and opens her red paper bag and draws from it her fallen hair. It is a great mass of dark wild hair. She holds it up to him. He appears not to understand. He stares at it.)* It is my hair. *(He continues to stare at her.)* When I awakened this morning it had fallen out, not all of it but a mass from the crown of my head that lay on the center of my pillow. I arose and in the greyish winter morning light of my room I stood staring at my hair, dazed by my sleeplessness, still shaken by nightmares of my mother. Was is true, yes, it was my hair. In the mirror I saw that, although my hair remained on both sides, clearly on the crown and at my temples my scalp was bare. *(She removes her black crown and shows him the top of her head.)*

FUNNYMAN. *(Staring at her.)* Why would your hair fall out? Is it because you are cruel? How could a black father haunt you so?

DUCHESS. He haunted my very conception. He was a wild black beast who raped my mother.

FUNNYMAN. He is a black Negro. *(Laughing.)*

DUCHESS. Ever since I can remember he's been in a nigger pose of agony. He is the wilderness. He speaks niggerly groveling about wanting to touch me with his black hand.

FUNNYMAN. How tormented and cruel you are.

DUCHESS. *(As if not comprehending.)* Yes, yes, the man's dark, very dark-skinned. He is the darkest, my father is the darkest, my mother is the lightest. I am in between. But my father is the darkest. My father is a nigger who drives me to misery. Any time spent with him evolves itself into suffering. He is a black man and the wilderness.

FUNNYMAN. How tormented and cruel you are.

DUCHESS. He is a nigger.

FUNNYMAN. And your mother, where is she?

DUCHESS. She is in the asylum. In the asylum bald. Her father was a white man. And she is in the asylum.

(He takes her in his arms. She responds wildly.)

BLACKOUT

KNOCKING is heard; it continues, then somewhere near the Center of the Stage a FIGURE *appears in the darkness, a large dark faceless* MAN *carrying a mask in his hand.*

MAN. It begins with the disaster of my hair. I awaken. My hair has fallen out, not all of it, but a mass from the crown of my head that lies on the center of my white pillow. I arise and in the greyish winter morning light of my room I stand staring at my hair, dazed by sleeplessness, still shaken by nightmares of my mother. Is it true? Yes. It is my hair. In the mirror I see that although my hair remains on both sides, clearly on the crown and at my temples my scalp is bare. And in my sleep I had been visited by my bald crazy mother who comes to me crying, calling me to her bedside. She lies on the bed watching the strands of her own hair fall out. Her hair fell out after she married and she spent her days lying on the bed watching the strands fall from her scalp, covering the bedspread until she was bald and admitted to the hospital. Black man, black man, my mother says, I never should have let a black man put his hands on me. She comes to me, he bald skull shining. Black diseases, Sarah, she says. Black diseases. I run. She follows me, her bald skull shining. That is the beginning.

BLACKOUT

SCENE: *Queen's Chamber.*

Her hair is in a small pile on the bed and in a small pile on the floor, several other small piles of hair are scattered about her and her white gown is covered with fallen out hair. QUEEN VICTORIA *acts out the following scene: She awakens (in pantomime) and discovers her hair has fallen. It is on her pillow. She arises and stands at the side of the bed with her back toward us, staring at hair. The* DUCHESS *enters the room, comes around, standing behind* VICTORIA, *and they stare at the hair.* VICTORIA *picks up a mirror. The* DUCHESS *then picks up a mirror and looks at her own hair. She opens the red paper bag that she is carrying and takes out her hair, attempting to place it back on her head (for unlike* VICTORIA, *she does not wear her headpiece now.) The LIGHTS remain on. The unidentified* MAN *returns out of the darkness and speaks. He carries the mask.*

MAN. *(Patrice Lumumba.)* I am a nigger of two generations. I am Patrice Lumumba. I am a nigger of two generations. I am the black shadow that haunted my mother's conception. I belong to the generation born at the turn of the century and the generation born before the depression. At present I reside in New York City in a brownstone in the West Nineties. I am an English major at a city college. My nigger father majored in social work, so did my mother. I am a student and have occasional work in libraries. But mostly I spend my vile days preoccupied with the placement and geometric position of words on paper. I write poetry filling white page after white page with imitations of Sitwell. It is my vile dream to live in rooms with European antiques and my statue of Queen Victoria, photographs of Roman ruins, walls of books, a piano and oriental carpets and to eat my meals on a white glass table. It is also my nigger dream for my friends to eat their meals on white glass tables and to live in rooms with European antiques, photographs of Roman ruins, pianos and oriental carpets. My friends will be white. I need them as an embankment to keep me from reflecting too much upon the fact that I am Patrice Lumumba who haunted my mother's conception. They are necessary for me to maintain recognition against myself. My white friends, like myself, will be shrewd intellectuals and anxious for death. Anyone's death. I will despise them as I do myself. For if I did not despise myself then my hair would not have fallen and if my hair had not fallen then I would not have bludgeoned my father's face with the ebony mask.

(The LIGHT remains on him. Before him a BALD HEAD is dropped on a wire, SOMEONE screams. Another wall is dropped, larger than the first one was. This one is near the front of the Stage facing thus. Throughout the following monologue, the CHAR-ACTERS: DUCHESS, VICTORIA, JESUS go back and forth. As they go in their backs are to us but the NEGRO faces us, speaking:)

I always dreamed of a day when my mother would smile at me. My father . . . his mother wanted him to be Christ. From the beginning in the lamp of their dark room she said—I want you to be Jesus, to walk in Genesis and save the race. You must return to Africa, find revelation in the midst of golden savannas, nim and white frankopenny trees, white stallions roaming under a blue sky, you must walk with a white dove and heal the race, heal the misery, take us off the cross. She stared at him anguished in the kerosene light . . . At dawn he watched her rise, kill a hen for him to eat at breakfast, then go to work down at the big house till dusk, till she died.

His father told him the race was no damn good. He hated his father and adored his mother. His mother didn't want him to marry my mother and sent a dead chicken to the wedding. I DON'T want you marrying that child, she wrote, she's not good enough for you, I want you to go to Africa. When they first married they lived in New York. Then they went to Africa where my mother fell out of love with my father. She didn't want him to save the black race and spent her days combing her hair. She would not let him touch her in their wedding bed and called him black. He is black of skin with dark eyes and a great dark square brow. Then in Africa he started to drink and came home drunk one night and raped my mother. The child from the union is me. I clung to my mother. Long after she went to the asylum I wove long dreams of her beauty, her straight hair and fair skin and grey eyes, so identical to mine. How it anguished him. I turned from him, nailing him on the cross, he said, dragging him through grass and nailing him on a cross until he bled. He pleaded with me to help him find Genesis, search for Genesis in the midst of golden savannas, nim and white frankopenny trees and white stallions roaming under a blue sky, help him search for the white doves, he wanted the black man to make a pure statement, he wanted the black man to rise from colonialism. But I sat in the room with my mother, sat by her bedside and helped her comb her straight black hair and wove long dreams of her beauty. She had long since begun to curse the place and spoke of herself trapped in blackness. She preferred the company of night owls. Only at night did she rise, walking in the garden among the trees with the owls. When I spoke to her she saw I was a black man's child and she preferred speaking to owls. Nights my father came from his school in the village struggling to embrace me. But I fled and hid under my mother's bed while she screamed of remorse. Her hair was falling badly and after a while we had to return to this country.

He tried to hang himself once. After my mother went to the asylum he had hallucinations, his mother threw a dead chicken at him, his father laughed and said the race was no damn good, my mother appeared in her nightgown screaming she had trapped herself in blackness. No white doves flew. He had left Africa and was again in New York. He lived in Harlem and no white doves flew. Sarah, Sarah, he would say to me, the soldiers are coming and a cross they are placing high on a tree and are dragging me through the grass and nailing me upon the cross. My blood is gushing. I wanted to live in Genesis in the midst of golden savannas, nim and white frankopenny trees and white stallions roaming under a blue sky. I wanted to walk with a white dove. I wanted to be a Christian. Now I am Judas. I betrayed my mother. I sent your mother to the asylum. I created a yellow child who hates me. And he tried to hang himself in a Harlem hotel.

BLACKOUT

(A BALD HEAD is dropped on a string. We hear LAUGHING.)

SCENE: *Duchess's place.*

The next scene is done in the Duchess of Hapsburg's place which is a chandeliered ballroom with SNOW falling, a black and white marble floor, a bench decorated with white flowers, all of this can be made of obviously fake materials as they would be in a funnyhouse. The DUCHESS is wearing a white dress and as in the previous scene a white headpiece with her kinky hair springing out from under it. In the scene are the DUCHESS and JESUS. JESUS enters the room, which is at first dark, then suddenly BRILLIANT, he starts to cry out at the DUCHESS, who is seated on a bench under the chandelier, and pulls his hair from the red paper bag holding it up for the DUCHESS to see.

JESUS. My hair. *(The DUCHESS does not speak, JESUS again screams.)* My hair. *(Holding the hair up, waiting for a reaction from the DUCHESS.)*

DUCHESS. *(As if oblivious.)* I have something I must show you. *(She goes quickly to shutters and darkens the room, returning standing before JESUS. She then slowly removes her headpiece and from under it takes a mass of her hair.)* When I awakened I found it fallen out, not all of it but a mass that lay on my white pillow. I could see, although my hair hung down at the sides, clearly on my white scalp it was missing.

(Her baldness is identical to JESUS'S.)

BLACKOUT

The LIGHTS come back up. They are BOTH *sitting on the bench examining each other's hair, running it through their fingers, then slowly the* DUCHESS *disappears behind the shutters and returns with a long red comb. She sits on the bench next to* JESUS *and starts to comb her remaining hair over her baldness. (This is done slowly.)* JESUS *then takes the comb and proceeds to do the same to the* DUCHESS *of Hapsburg's hair. After they finish they place the* DUCHESS'S *headpiece back on and we can see the strands of their hair falling to the floor.* JESUS *then lies down across the bench while the* DUCHESS *walks back and forth, the* KNOCKING *does not cease. They speak in unison as the* DUCHESS *walks about and* JESUS *lies on the bench in the falling snow, staring at the ceiling.*

DUCHESS and JESUS. *(Their hair is falling more now, they are both hideous.)* My father isn't going to let us alone. *(KNOCKING.)* Our father isn't going to let us alone, our father is the darkest of us all, my mother was the fairest, I am in between, but my father is the darkest of them all. He is a black man. Our father is the darkest of them all. He is a black man. My father is a dead man.

(Then they suddenly look up at each other and scream, the LIGHTS go to their heads and we see that they are totally bald. There is a KNOCKING. LIGHTS go to the stairs and the LANDLADY.)

LANDLADY. He wrote to her saying he loved her and asked her forgiveness. He begged her to take him off the cross *(He had dreamed she would.),* stop them from tormenting him, the one with the chicken and his cursing father. Her mother's hair fell out, the race's hair fell out because he left Africa, he said. He had tried to save them. She must embrace him. He said his existence depended on her embrace. He wrote her from Africa where he is creating his Christian center in the jungle and that is why he came here. I know that he wanted her to return there with him and not desert the race. He came to see her once before he tried to hang himself, appearing in the corridor of my apartment. I had let him in. I found him sitting on a bench in the hallway. He put out his hand to her, tried to take her in his arms, crying out—Forgiveness, Sarah, is it that you never will forgive me for being black? Sarah, I know you were a child of torment. But forgiveness. That was before his breakdown. Then, he wrote her and repeated that his mother hoped he would be Christ but he failed. He had married her mother because he could not resist the light. Yet, his mother from the beginning in the kerosene lamp of their dark rooms in Georgia said: I want you to be Jesus, to walk in Genesis and save the race, return to Africa, find revelation in the black. He went away.

But Easter morning, she got to feeling badly and went into Harlem to see him; the streets were filled with vendors selling lilies. He had checked out of that hotel. When she arrived back at my brownstone he was here, dressed badly, rather drunk, I had let him in again. He sat on a bench in the dark hallway, put out his hand to her, trying to take her in his arms, crying out—forgiveness, Sarah, forgiveness for my being black, Sarah. I know you are a child of torment. I know on dark winter afternoons you sit alone weaving stories of your mother's beauty. But Sarah, answer me, don't turn away, Sarah. Forgive my blackness. She would not answer. He put out his hand to her. She ran past him on the stairs, left him there with his hand out to me, repeating his past, saying his mother hoped he would be

Christ. From the beginning in the kerosene lamp of their dark rooms, she said, "Wally, I want you to be Jesus, to walk in Genesis and save the race. You must return to Africa, Wally, find revelation in the midst of golden savannas, nim and white frankopenny trees and white stallions roaming under a blue sky. Wally, you must find the white dove and heal the pain of the race, heal the misery of the black man, Wally, take us off the cross, Wally." In the kerosene light she stared at me anguished from her old Negro face—but she ran past him leaving him. And now he is dead, she says, now he is dead. He left Africa and now Patrice Lumumba is dead.

(The next scene is enacted back in the DUCHESS *of Hapsburg's place.* JESUS *is still in the Duchess's chamber, apparently he has fallen asleep and as we see him he awakens with the* DUCHESS *by his side, and sits here as in a trance. He rises terrified and speaks.)*

JESUS. Through my apocalypses and my raging sermons I have tried so to escape him, through God Almighty I have tried to escape being black. *(He then appears to rouse himself from his thoughts and calls:)* Duchess, Duchess. *(He looks about for her, there is no answer. He gets up slowly, walks back into the darkness and there we see that she is hanging on the chandelier, her bald head suddenly drops to the floor and she falls upon* JESUS. *He screams.)* I am going to Africa and kill this black man named Patrice Lumumba. Why? Because all my life I believed my Holy Father to be God, but now I know that my father is a black man. I have no fear for whatever I do, I will do in the name of God, I will do in the name of Albert Saxe Coburg, in the name of Victoria, Queen Victoria

Regina, the monarch of England, I will.

BLACKOUT

SCENE: *In the jungle, RED SUN, FLYING THINGS, wild
black grass. The effect of the jungle is that it, unlike
the other scenes, is over the entire stage. In time this
is the longest scene in the play and is played the
slowest, as the slow, almost standstill stages of a
dream. By lighting the desired effect would be—
suddenly the jungle has overgrown the chambers and
all the other places with a violence and a dark
brightness, a grim yellowness.*

JESUS *is the first to appear in the center of the jungle
darkness. Unlike in previous scenes, he has a nimbus
above his head. As they each successively appear,
they all too have nimbuses atop their heads in a
manner to suggest that they are saviours.*

JESUS. I always believed my father to be God.

(Suddenly they all appear in various parts of the jungle.
PATRICE LUMUMBA, *the* DUCHESS, VICTORIA,
*wandering about speaking at once. Their speeches
are mixed and repeated by one another:)*

ALL. He never tires of the journey, he who is the
darkest one, the darkest one of them all. My mother looked
like a white woman, hair as straight as any white woman's. I
am yellow but he is black, the darkest one of us all. How I
hoped he was dead, yet he never tires of the journey. It was
because of him that my mother died because she let a black

man put his hands on her. Why does he keep returning? He keeps returning forever, keeps returning and returning and he is my father. He is a black Negro. They told me my Father was God but my father is black. He is my father. I am tied to a black Negro. He returned when I lived in the south back in the twenties, when I was a child, he returned. Before I was born at the turn of the century, he haunted my conception, diseased my birth . . . killed my mother. He killed the light. My mother was the lightest one. I am bound to him unless, of course, he should die.

But he is dead.

And he keeps returning. Then he is not dead.

Then he is not dead.

Yet, he is dead, but dead he comes knocking at my door.

(This is repeated several times, finally reaching a loud pitch and then ALL *rushing about the grass. They stop and stand perfectly still.* ALL *speaking tensely at various times in a chant.)*

I see him. The black ugly thing is sitting in his hallway, surrounded by his ebony masks, surrounded by the blackness of himself. My mother comes into the room. He is there with his hand out to me, groveling, saying—Forgiveness, Sarah, is it that you will never forgive me for being black.

Forgiveness, Sarah, I know you are a nigger of torment.

Why? Christ would not rape anyone.

You will never forgive me for being black.

Wild beast. Why did you rape my mother? Black beast, Christ would not rape anyone.

He is in grief from that black anguished face of his. Then at once the room will grow bright and my mother will come toward me smiling while I stand before his face and bludgeon him with an ebony head.

Forgiveness, Sarah, I know you are a nigger of torment.

(Silence. Then they suddenly begin to laugh and shout as though they are in victory. They continue for some minutes running about laughing and shouting.)

BLACKOUT

Another WALL drops. There is a white plaster statue of Queen Victoria which represents the Negro's room in the brownstone, the room appears near the staircase highly lit and small. The main prop is the statue but a bed could be suggested. The figure of Victoria is a sitting figure, one of astonishing repulsive whiteness, suggested by dusty volumes of books and old yellowed walls.

The Negro SARAH *is standing perfectly still, we hear the KNOCKING, the LIGHTS come on quickly, her* FATHER'S *black figure with bludgeoned hands rushes upon her, the LIGHT GOES BLACK and we see her hanging in the room.*

LIGHTS come on the laughing LANDLADY. *And at the same time remain on the hanging figure of the* NEGRO.

LANDLADY. The poor bitch has hung herself. *(*FUNNYMAN RAYMOND *appears from his room at the commotion.)* The poor bitch has hung herself.

RAYMOND. *(Observing her hanging figure.)* She was a funny little liar.

LANDLADY. *(Informing him.)* Her father hung himself in a Harlem hotel when Patrice Lumumba died.

RAYMOND. Her father never hung himself in a Harlem hotel when Patrice Lumumba was murdered. I know the man. He is a doctor, married to a white whore. He lives in the city in rooms with European antiques, photographs of Roman ruins, walls of books and oriental carpets. Her father is a nigger who eats his meals on a white glass table.

END

The OWL ANSWERS

Characters

SHE who is CLARA PASSMORE who is the VIRGIN MARY who is the BASTARD who is the OWL.

BASTARD'S BLACK MOTHER who is the REVEREND'S WIFE who is ANNE BOLEYN.

GODDAM FATHER who is the RICHEST WHITE MAN IN THE TOWN who is the DEAD WHITE FATHER who is REVEREND PASSMORE.

THE WHITE BIRD who is REVEREND PASSMORE'S CANARY who is GOD'S DOVE.

THE NEGRO MAN.

SHAKESPEARE, CHAUCER, WILLIAM THE CONQUEROR.

The characters change slowly back and forth into and out of themselves, leaving some garment from their previous selves upon them always to remind us of the nature of She who is Clara Passmore who is the Virgin Mary who is the Bastard who is the Owl's world.

Original production by Lucille Lortel, at The White Barn Theatre, Westport, Connecticut, 1965, directed by Michael Kahn.

SCENE: *The scene is a New York subway is the Tower of London is a Harlem hotel room is St. Peter's. The scene is shaped like a subway car. The sounds are subway sounds and the main props of a subway are visible—poles. Two seats on the scene are like seats on the subway, the seat in which* SHE WHO IS *sits and* NEGRO MAN'S *seat.*

Seated is a plain, pallid NEGRO WOMAN, *wearing a cotton summer dress that is too long, a pair of white wedged sandals. She sits staring into space. She is* CLARA PASSMORE *who is the* VIRGIN MARY *who is the* BASTARD *who is the* OWL. SHE WHO IS *speaks in a soft voice as a Negro schoolteacher from Savannah would.* SHE WHO IS *carries white handkerchiefs,* SHE WHO IS *carries notebooks that throughout the play like the handkerchiefs fall. She will pick them up, glance frenziedly at a page from a notebook, be distracted, place the notebooks in a disorderly pile, drop them again, etc. The scene should lurch, lights flash, gates slam. When* THEY *come in and exit they move in the manner of people on a train, too there is the noise of the train, the sound of moving steel on the track. The* WHITE BIRD'S *wings should flutter loudly. The gates, the High Altar, the ceiling and the Dome are like St. Peter's, the walls are like the Tower of London.*

The music which SHE WHO IS *hears at the most violent times of her experience should be Haydn's "Concerto for Horn in D" (Third Movement).*

Objects on the stage (beards, wigs, faces) should be used in the manner that people use everyday objects such as spoons or newspapers. The Tower Gate should be black, yet slam like a subway door. The GATES SLAM. Four people enter from different directions. They are SHAKESPEARE, WILLIAM THE CON-QUEROR, CHAUCER *and* ANNE BOLEYN. *They are dressed in costumes of Shakespeare, William the Conqueror, Chaucer and Anne Boleyn but too they are strangers entering a subway on a summer night, too they are the guards in the Tower of London. Their lines throughout the play are not spoken specifically by one person but by all or part of them.*

THEY. Bastard. *(They start at a distance, eventually crowding her. Their lines are spoken coldly.* SHE WHO IS *is only a prisoner to them.)*

You are not his ancestor.

Keep her locked there, guard.

Bastard.

SHE. You must let me go down to the chapel to see him. He is my father.

THEY. Your father? *(Jeering.)*

SHE. He is my father.

THEY. Keep her locked there, guard.

*(*SHAKESPEARE *crosses to gate and raises hands. There is a SLAM as if great door is being closed.)*

SHE. We came this morning. We were visiting the place of our ancestors, my father and I. We had a lovely morning, we rose in darkness, took a taxi past Hyde Park through the Marble Arch to Buckingham Palace, we had our morning tea at Lyons then came out to the Tower. We were wandering about the gardens, my father leaning on my arm, speaking of you, William the Conqueror. My father loved you, William. . . .

       THEY. *(Interrupting.)* If you are his ancestor why are you a Negro?

Yes, why is it you are a Negro if you are his ancestor?

Keep her locked there.

       SHE. You must let me go down to the Chapel to see him.

(SUBWAY STOPS. Doors open. CHAUCER exits. ANNE BOLEYN and WILLIAM THE CONQUEROR remain staring at HER. CHAUCER and SHAKESPEARE return carrying a stiff dead man in a black suit. The most noticeable thing about him is his hair, long, silky, white hair that hangs as they bring him through the gate and place him at her feet.)

       THEY. Here is your father.

(They then all exit through various gate entrances. SHE picks up the dead man, drags him to a dark, carved high-backed chair on the Right. At the same time a dark NEGRO MAN, with a dark suit and black glasses on, enters from the Right gate and sits on the other subway seat. Flashing, movement, slamming the gate. The scene revolves one and one-quarter turns as next action takes place. The NEGRO MAN sits up very straight and proceeds to watch SHE WHO IS. Until he speaks to her he watches her constantly with a wild, cold stare. The DEAD FATHER appears dead. He is dead. Yet as SHE watches, he moves and comes to life. The DEAD FATHER removes his hair, takes off his white face, from the chair he takes a white church robe and puts it on. Beneath his white hair is dark Negro hair. He is

now REVEREND PASSMORE. *After he dresses he looks about as if something is missing. SUBWAY STOPS, doors open.* FATHER *exits and returns with a gold bird cage that hangs near the chair and a white battered Bible. Very matter-of-factly he sits down in the chair, stares for a moment at the cage, then opens the Bible, starting to read.* SHE *watches, highly distracted, until he falls asleep. Scene revolves one turn as* ANNE BOLEYN *throws red rice at* SHE WHO IS *and the* DEAD FATHER *who is now* REVEREND PASSMORE. *They see her.* SHE *exits and returns with a great black gate and places the gate where the pole is.* SHE WHO IS *runs to* ANNE BOLEYN.)

SHE. Anne, Anne Boleyn. (*Throws rice upon* SHE WHO IS CLARA PASSMORE *who is the* VIRGIN MARY *who is the* BASTARD *who is the* OWL.) Anne, you know so much of love, won't you help me? They took my father away and will not let me see him. They locked me in this tower and I can see them taking his body across to the Chapel to be buried and see his white hair hanging down. Let me into the Chapel. He is my blood father. I am almost white, am I not? Let me into St. Paul's Chapel. Let me please go down to St. Paul's Chapel. I am his daughter. (ANNE *appears to listen quite attentively but her reply is to turn into the* BASTARD'S BLACK MOTHER. *She takes off part of her own long dress and puts on a rose-colored, cheap lace dress. While she does this there is a terrific SCREECH.* SHE WHO IS'S *reaction is to run back to her subway seat. She drops her notebooks. The* BASTARD'S BLACK MOTHER *opens her arms to* SHE WHO IS. SHE *returns to the gate.*) Anne. (*As if trying to bring back* ANNE BOLEYN.)

BBM (BASTARD'S BLACK MOTHER). *(Laughs and throws a white bridal bouquet at her.)* Clara, I am not Anne. I am the Bastard's Black Mother, who cooked for somebody. *(Still holding out her arms, she kneels by the gate, her kinky hair awry. Eyes closed, she stares upward, praying. Suddenly she stops praying and pulls at* SHE WHO IS *through the gate.)*

(The WHITE BIRD, *with very loud fluttering wings, flies down from St. Peter's Dome and goes into the cage.* REVEREND PASSMORE *gets up and closes the cage door.)*

SHE. Anne, it is I.

BBM. Clara, you were conceived by your Goddam Father who was The Richest White Man in the Town and somebody that cooked for him. That's why you're an owl. *(Laughs.)* That's why when I see you, Mary, I cry. I cry when I see Marys, cry for their deaths.

*(*WHITE BIRD *flies.* REVEREND *reads. The* BASTARD'S BLACK MOTHER *stands at the gate, watches, then takes off rose lace dress and black face [beneath her black face is a more pallid Negro face], pulls down her hair, longer dark hair, and puts on a white dress. From a fold in the dress she takes out a picture of Christ, then kneels and stares upward. She is the* REVEREND'S WIFE. *While she does this the scene revolves one turn.)*

REVEREND'S WIFE. *(Kneeling.* REVEREND *stands and watches her.* REVEREND'S WIFE *takes a vial from her gown and holds it up.)* These are the fruits of my maidenhead, owl blood Clara who is the Bastard Clara

Passmore to whom we gave our name, see the Owl blood, that is why I cry when I see Marys, cry for their deaths, Owl Mary Passmore.

(SHE *gets up, exits from a side gate.* SUBWAY STOPS, *gates open, they come in, gates close.* SUBWAY STARTS. SHE WHO IS *goes to the* REVEREND *as if to implore him. He then changes into the* DEAD FATHER, *resuming his dirty white hair.* THEY *stand about.*)

SHE. Dear Father, My Goddam Father who was the Richest White Man in the Town, who is Dead Father—you know that England is the home of dear Chaucer, Dickens and dearest Shakespeare. Winters we spent here at the Tower, our chambers were in the Queen's House, summers we spent at Stratford with dearest Shakespeare. It was all so lovely. I spoke to Anne Boleyn, Dead Father. She knows so much of love and suffering and I believe she is going to try to help me. (*Takes a sheaf of papers from her notebooks; they fall to the floor.*) Communications, all communications to get you the proper burial, the one you deserve in St. Paul's Chapel, they are letting you rot, my Goddam Father who was the Richest White Man in the Town—they are letting you rot in that town in Georgia. I haven't been able to see the king. I'll speak again to Anne Boleyn. She knows so much of love. (*Shows the papers to the* DEAD FATHER *who sits with his hair hanging down, dead, at which point scene revolves clock-wise one-half turn. There are* SCREECHES, *and bird flaps wings. The* REVEREND'S WIFE *enters and prays at gate.*)

DEAD FATHER. If you are my ancestor why are you a Negro, Bastard? What is a Negro doing at the Tower of London, staying at the Queen's House? Clara, I am your Goddam Father who was the Richest White Man in the

Town and you are a schoolteacher in Savannah who spends her summers in Teachers College. You are not my ancestor. You are my bastard. Keep her locked there, William.

SHE. (*They stare at her like passengers on a subway, standing, holding the hand straps.*) We were wandering about the garden, you leaning on my arm, speaking of William the Conqueror. We sat on the stone bench to rest, when we stood up you stumbled and fell onto the walk— dead. Dead. I called the guard. Then I called the Warder and told him my father had just died, that we had been visiting London together, the place of our ancestors and all the lovely English, and my father just died. (*She reaches out to touch him.*)

DEAD FATHER. You are not my ancestor.

SHE. They jeered. They brought me to this tower and locked me up. I can see they're afraid of me. From the tower I saw them drag you across the court . . . your hair hanging down. They have taken off your shoes and you are stiff. You are stiff. (*Touches him.*) My dear father. (*MUSIC: Haydn.*)

DEAD FATHER. Daughter of somebody that cooked for me. (*Smiles. He then ignores* SHE WHO IS, *changes into the* REVEREND, *takes the Bible and starts to read. The* WHITE BIRD *flies into the cage. Wings flutter. The* REVEREND'S WIFE *prays, lights a candle. The* REVEREND *watches the* BIRD. REVEREND'S WIFE *then puts on her black face, rose dress. Some of the red rice has fallen near her, she says, "Oww," and starts to peck at it like a bird.* SHE WHO IS *wanders about, then comes to speak to the* BASTARD'S BLACK MOTHER *who remains seated like an owl. END MUSIC.*)

SHE. It was you, the Bastard's Black Mother, who told me. I asked you where did Mr. William Mattheson's family come from and you, my Black Mother, said: I believe his father came from England. England, I said. England is the Brontës' home. Did you know, Black Bastard's Mother, who cooked for somebody, in the Reverend's parlor—there in a glass bookcase are books and England is the home of Chaucer, Dickens and Shakespeare. Black Mother who cooked for somebody, Mr. William Mattheson died today. I was at the College. The Reverend's Wife called me, Clara who is the Bastard who is the Virgin Mary who is the Owl. Clara, who is the Bastard who is the Virgin Mary who is the Owl, Clara, she said, the Reverend told me to call you and tell you Mr. William Mattheson died today or it was yesterday he died yesterday. It was yesterday. The Reverend told me to tell you it was yesterday he died and it is today they're burying him. Clara who is the Bastard, you mustn't come. Don't do anything foolish like come to the funeral, Mary. You've always been such a fool about that white man, Clara. But I am coming, the Black Bastard's Mother. I am coming, my Goddam Father who was the Richest White Man in Jacksonville, Georgia. When I arrive in London, I'll go out to Buckingham Palace, see the Thames at dusk and Big Ben. I'll go for lovely walks through Hyde Park, and to innumerable little tearooms with great bay windows and white tablecloths on little white tables and order tea. I will go all over and it will be June. Then I'll go out to the Tower to see you, my father.

(SUBWAY STOPS. Doors open. THEY enter.)

THEY. If you are his ancestor, what are you doing on the subway at night looking for men?
What are you doing looking for men to take to a hotel room in Harlem?

Negro men?
Negro men, Clara Passmore?

(GATES CLOSE, SUBWAY STARTS, BIRD'S wings flap.)

SHE. *(Runs to the BIRD.)* My dead father's bird: God's Dove. My father died today.

BIRD. *(Mocking.)* My father died today, God's Dove.

SHE. He was the Richest White Man in our Town. I was conceived by him and somebody that cooked for him.

BIRD. What are you doing in the Tower of London then?

(The REVEREND becomes the DEAD FATHER who comes forward, pantomimes catching the BIRD, puts him in the cage, shuts the door.)

SHE. My father. *(He turns, stares at her and comes toward her and dies. There is a CLANG.)* What were you saying to William, my father, you loved William so? *(She holds him in her arms. He opens his eyes.)*

DEAD FATHER. *(Waking.)* Mary, at last you are coming to me. *(MUSIC: Haydn.)*

SHE. I am not Mary, I am Clara, your daughter, Reverend Passmore—I mean Dead Father. *(BIRD flies in the cage.)*

DEAD FATHER. Yes, my Mary, you are coming into my world. You are filled with dreams of my world. I sense it all.

(Scene revolves counterclockwise one and one-quarter turns. LIGHTS FLASH. SHE WHO IS, trying to escape, runs into NEGRO MAN.)

NEGRO MAN. At last you are coming to me. *(Smiles.)*

DEAD FATHER. Mary, come in here for eternity. Are you confused? Yes, I can see you are confused. *(*THEY *come on.)*

THEY. Are you confused? *(One of them,* CHAUCER, *is now dressed as the* REVEREND. *He comes, falls down onto the empty high-backed chair and sits staring into the Bible.)*

DEAD FATHER. So at last you are coming to me, Bastard.

*(*BASTARD'S BLACK MOTHER *exits from gate, returns, part owl with owl feathers upon her, dragging a great dark bed through the gate.)*

BBM. Why be confused? The Owl was your beginning, Mary. *(There is a GREAT CLANG. Begins to build with the bed and feathers the High Altar. Feathers fly.)*

SHE. He came to me in the outhouse, he came to me under the porch, in the garden, in the fig tree. He told me you are an owl, ow, oww, I am your beginning, ow. You belong here with us owls in the fig tree, not to somebody that cooks for your Goddam Father, oww, and I ran to the outhouse in the night crying oww. Bastard they say, the people in the town all say Bastard, but I—I belong to God and the owls, ow, and I sat in the fig tree. My Goddam Father is the Richest White Man in the Town, but I belong to the owls, till Reverend Passmore adopted me they all said Bastard . . . then my father was a reverend. He preached in the Holy Baptist Church on the top of the hill, on the top of the Holy Hill and everybody in the town knew then my name was Mary. My father was the Baptist preacher and I was Mary. *(SUBWAY STOPS, GATES OPEN.* THEY *enter.*

GATES CLOSE. SUBWAY STARTS. SHE *sits next to* NEGRO MAN.) I who am the ancestor of Shakespeare, Chaucer and William the Conqueror, I went to London— the Queen Elizabeth. London. They all said who ever heard of anybody going to London but I went. I stayed in my cabin the whole crossing, solitary. I was the only Negro there. I read books on subjects like the History of London, the Life of Anne Boleyn, Mary Queen of Scots and Sonnets. When I wasn't in the cabin I wrapped myself in a great sweater and sat over the dark desks in the writing room and wrote my father. I wrote him every day of my journey. I met my father once when my mother took me to visit him and we had to go into the back door of his house. I was married once briefly. On my wedding day the Reverend's Wife came to me and said when I see Marys I cry for their deaths, when I see brides, Clara, I cry for their deaths. But the past years I've spent teaching alone in Savannah. And alone I'm almost thirty-four, I who am the ancestor of somebody that cooked for somebody and William the Conqueror. (DEAD FATHER *rises, goes to her, then dies again. GREAT CLANG.* BLACK MOTHER *shakes a rattle at* SHE. SHE *screams at the* DEAD FATHER *and the* MOTHER.) You must know how it is to be filled with yearning.

(THEY *laugh.* MOTHER *bangs at the bed.)*

     NEGRO MAN. *(Touches her.)* And what exactly do you yearn for?
     SHE. You know.
     NEGRO MAN. No, what is it?
     SHE. I want what I think everyone wants.
     NEGRO MAN. And what is that?
     SHE. I don't know. Love or something, I guess.
     NEGRO MAN. Out there Owl?

DEAD FATHER. In St. Paul's Chapel Owl?

THEY. Keep her locked there, guard. *(GREAT CLANG.)*

BBM. Is this love to come from out there?

SHE. I don't know what you mean.

DEAD FATHER. I know you don't.

THEY. We know you don't.

SHE. Call me Mary.

NEGRO MAN. Mary?

THEY. Keep her locked there.

DEAD FATHER. If you are Mary what are you doing in the Tower of London?

NEGRO MAN. Mary?

(The REVEREND *gets up, goes to chair, puts on robe, sits. The* BASTARD'S BLACK MOTHER *reappears on the other side of the gate, owl feathers about her, bearing a vial, still wearing the long black hair of the* REVEREND'S WIFE.)

BBM. When I see sweet Marys I cry for their deaths, Clara. The Reverend took my maidenhead and I am not a Virgin anymore and that is why you must be Mary, always be Mary, Clara.

SHE. Mama. (BLACK MOTHER *rises. Steps in costume of* ANNE BOLEYN.) Mama. *(Watches her change to* ANNE BOLEYN. *They watch.)*

BBM. What are you doing on the subway if you are his ancestor?

*(*ANNE *makes circular cross around stage until* SHE *is back in same position* SHE *started at.)*

SHE. I am Clara Passmore. I am not His ancestor. I

ride, look for men to take to a Harlem hotel room, to love, dress them as my father, beg to take me.

THEY. Take you?

SHE. Yes, take me, Clara Passmore.

THEY. Take you, Bastard?

SHE. There is a bed there.

(The WHITE BIRD *laughs like the mother.)*

WILL. And do they take you?

SHE. No, William.

WILL. No?

SHE. Something happens.

WILL. Happens?

CHAUCER. Happens?

SHE. Something strange always happens, Chaucer.

CHAUCER. Where?

SHE. In the hotel room. It's how I've passed my summer in New York, nights I come to the subway, look for men. It's how I've passed my summer. If they would only take me! But something strange happens.

ANNE. Take you, Mary. Why, Mary? *(ANNE has now reached gate.)*

*(*BLACK MOTHER *steps out of costume, crosses to bed.* SHE *talks to* ANNE *as if she were there.)*

SHE. Anne, you must help me. They, my Black Mother and my Goddam Father and the Reverend and his wife, they and the teachers at the school where I teach, and Professor Johnson, the principal to whom I'm engaged, they all say, "London, who in the hell ever heard of anybody going to London?" Of course I shouldn't go. They said I had lost my mind, read so much, buried myself in my books.

They said I should stay and teach summer school to the kids up from Oglethorpe. But I went. All the way from Piccadilly Circus out there in the black taxi, my cold hands were colder than ever. Then it happened. No sooner than I left the taxi and passed down a grey walk through a dark gate and into a garden where there were black ravens on the grass when I broke down. I broke down and started to cry, oh the Tower, winters in Queen's House, right in front of everybody. People came and stared. I was the only Negro there. The Guard came and stared, the ravens flew and finally a man with a black hat on helped me out through the gate into the street. I am never going back, Anne. Anne, I am never going back. I will not go.

(SUBWAY STOPS, GATES OPEN.)

THEY. Keep her locked there, guard.

(LIGHT comes through gates as if opened. SHE makes crown of paper, and places on NEGRO MAN'S head.)

SHE. God, do you see it? Do you see? They are opening the cell door to let me go.

NEGRO MAN. See it, Mary?

SHE. They are opening the cell door to let me go down to St. Paul's Chapel where I am yearning to go. Do you see it?

NEGRO MAN. Love? Love Mary?

SHE. Love?

NEGRO MAN. Love in St. Paul's Chapel? *(He tries to grab at her.)*

SHE. No, no, the love that exists between you and me. Do you see it?

NEGRO MAN. Love Mary? *(He takes her hand, with*

his other hand, he tries to undress her.)

SHE. Love God.

NEGRO MAN. Love Mary?

SHE. Love God.

THEY. *(Simultaneously.)* Bastard, you are not His ancestor, you are not God's ancestor. *(There is a SCREECH as* THEY *bring the* DEAD FATHER *and leave him at her feet.)*

NEGRO MAN. Love Mary?

SHE. Love God. Yes.

BBM. *(Calls.)* Clara. Clara. *(The* REVEREND *watching.)*

THEY. Open the door. Let her go, let her go, guards. Open the cell door. *(*THEY *exit, leaving the gates open.)*

*(*NEGRO MAN *will not release* SHE WHO IS *Clara who is the Bastard who is the Virgin Mary who is the Owl.)*

SHE. Go away. Go away. *(The* NEGRO MAN *will not release her.)*

(The REVEREND'S WIFE *goes on building the High Altar with owl feathers, prays, builds, prays, stops, holds out her hand to* SHE WHO IS, *puts up candles, puts up owl feathers, laughs, puts more candles on the High Altar.)*

REVEREND'S WIFE. *(Calls.)* Owl, come sit by me. *(The* REVEREND'S WIFE *does not look at* SHE WHO IS, *but rather stares feverishly upward, her gestures possessing the fervent quality of Biblical images. Sitting on the High Altar, she holds one of her hands over her shoulder as though she drew near the fingers of a deity. Suddenly her hand reaches inside her gown and she pulls up a butcher knife.)* Clara. *(Staring upward, holding the knife.)*

SHE. Yes, the Reverend's Wife who came to me on my wedding day and said I cry for the death of brides. Yes?

REVEREND'S WIFE. I told the Reverend if he ever came near me again . . . *(She turns the butcher knife around.)* Does he not know I am Mary, Christ's bride? What does he think? Does he think I am like your black mother who was the biggest whore in town? He must know I'm Mary. Only Mary would marry the Reverend Passmore of the church on the top of the Holy Hill. *(Turns the knife around, staring at it.* SHE *is leaving with* NEGRO MAN. REVEREND'S WIFE *is pulling her.)* We adopted you, took you from your bastard birth, Owl.

> *(*SHE *and* NEGRO MAN *exit. GATES CLOSE. SUBWAY STARTS.* REVEREND'S WIFE *drags bed onto Center Stage. She enters with* NEGRO MAN *Down Center.)*

SHE. Home, God, we're home. Did you know we came from England, God? It's the Brontës' home too. Winters we spent here at the Tower. Our chambers were in the Queen's House. Summers we spent at Stratford. It was so lovely. God, do you remember the loveliness?

> *(LIGHTS FLASH. Scene revolves clockwise one and one-quarter turns.* BIRD *flaps wings. LIGHT comes up on him.)*

BIRD. If you are the Virgin, what are you doing with this Negro in a Harlem hotel room? Mary?

SHE. My name is Clara Passmore.

BIRD. Mary. *(*WHITE BIRD *laughs like the* MOTHER. *The* REVEREND'S WIFE *lights candles.)*

NEGRO MAN. *(Going to her.)* What is it?

SHE. Call me Mary, God.

NEGRO MAN. Mary?

SHE. God, do you remember the loveliness?

REVEREND'S WIFE. *(Lights more candles and moves closer with the butcher knife, calling:)* Clara. *(The* BIRD *flies wildly, the* REVEREND *sits in the chair reading the white tattered Bible.)*

NEGRO MAN. What is it? What is it? What is wrong? *(He tries to undress her. Underneath her body is black. He throws off the crown she has placed on him. She is wildly trying to get away from him.)* What is it? *(The* WHITE BIRD *flies toward them and about the green room.)* Are you sick?

SHE. *(Smiles.)* No, God. *(She is in a trance.)* No, I am not sick. I only have a dream of love. A dream. Open the cell door and let me go down to St. Paul's Chapel. *(The blue crepe shawl is half about her. She shows the* NEGRO MAN *her notebooks, from which a mass of papers fall. She crazily tries to gather them up. During this* SHE *walks around bed. He follows her.)* Communications, God, communications, letters to my father. I am making it into my thesis. I write my father every day of the year.

God, I who am the Bastard who is the Virgin Mary who is the Owl, I came here this morning with my father. We were visiting England, the place of our ancestors, my father and I who am the Bastard who is the Virgin Mary who is the Owl. We had a lovely morning. We rose in darkness, took a taxi past Hyde Park, through the Marble Arch to Buckingham Palace. We had our morning tea at Lyons and then we came out to the Tower.

And I started to cry and a man with a black hat on helped me out of the gate to the street. I was the only Negro here.

They took him away and would not let me see him. They who are my Black Mother and my Goddam Father locked me in the fig tree and took his body away and his white hair hung down.

Now they, my Black Mother and my Goddam Father who pretend to be Chaucer, Shakespeare and Eliot and all my beloved English, come to my cell and stare and I can see they despise me and I despise them.

They are dragging his body across the green his white hair hanging down. They are taking off his shoes and he is stiff. I must get into the chapel to see him. I must. He is my blood father. God, let me into his burial. *(He grabs her Down Center.* SHE, *kneeling.)* I call God and the Owl answers. *(Softer.)* It haunts my Tower calling, its feathers are blowing against the cell wall, speckled in the garden on the fig tree, it comes, feathered, great hollow-eyed with yellow skin and yellow eyes, the flying bastard. From my Tower I keep calling and the only answer is the Owl, God. *(Pause. Stands.)* I am only yearning for our kingdom, God.

(The WHITE BIRD *flies back into the cage,* REVEREND *reads smiling, the* DEAD FATHER *lies on cell floor. The* MOTHER, *now part the black mother and part the* REVEREND'S WIFE *in a white dress, wild kinky hair, part feathered, comes closer to* CLARA.)

MOTHER. Owl in the fig tree, owl under the house, owl in outhouse. *(Calling cheerfully the way one would call a child, kissing* SHE WHO IS.) There is a way from owldom. *(Kissing her again.)* Clara who is the Bastard who is the Virgin who is the Owl.

SHE. *(Goes to* MOTHER.) My Black Mother who cooked for somebody who is the Reverend's Wife. Where is Anne Boleyn?

MOTHER. Owl in the fig tree, do you know it? Do you? Do you know the way to St. Paul's Chapel, Clara? *(Takes her hand.)* I do. Kneel, Mary, by the gate and pray with me who is your black mother who is Christ's Bride. *(She holds up the butcher knife.)* Kneel by the High Altar and pray with me. *(They kneel; she smiles.)* Do you know it, Clara, do you, Clara Bastard? *(Kisses her.)* Clara, I know the way to St. Paul's Chapel. I know the way to St. Paul's Chapel, Clara.

(MOTHER lifts knife. She stabs herself. At this moment, BIRD flaps wings, scene moves counterclockwise one turn. There is a SCREECH of a SUBWAY. Then the Haydn plays. When revolve stops, NEGRO MAN tries to kiss HER and pin HER down on bed. SHE is fighting him off. The WHITE BIRD descends steps.)

SHE. God, say, "You know I love you, Mary, yes, I love you. That love is the oldest, purest testament in my heart." Say, "Mary, it was a testament imprinted on my soul long before the world began. I pray to you, Mary." God, say, "Mary, I pray to you. Darling, come to my kingdom. Mary, leave owldom—come to my kingdom. I am awaiting you." *(The NEGRO MAN tries again to kiss HER. The WHITE BIRD picks up the DEAD MOTHER and takes her to the top of St. Peter's Dome. They remain there, watching down. The REVEREND reads the Bible, smiling.)*
NEGRO MAN. What is wrong?
SHE. Wrong, God?
NEGRO MAN. God?
SHE. Wrong, God?
NEGRO MAN. God? *(They are upon the burning High Altar. He tries to force her down, yet at the same time he is frightened by her. The DEAD FATHER who has been holding the candles, smiles.)*
SHE. Negro! *(MUSIC ENDS.)* Keep her locked there, guard. *(They struggle.)* I cry for the death of Marys.

(They struggle. SHE *screeches.)* Negro! *(She tries to get out of the room, but he will not let her go.)* Let me go to St. Paul's Chapel. Let me go down to see my Goddam Father who was the Richest White Man in the Town. *(They struggle, he is frightened now.)* God, God, call me, Mary. *(*SHE *screeches louder.)* God!! *(Suddenly she breaks away, withdraws the butcher knife, still with blood and feathers upon it, and very quickly tries to attack him, holds the knife up, aiming it at him, but then dropping it just as suddenly in a gesture of wild weariness. He backs farther. She falls down onto the side of the burning bed. The* NEGRO MAN *backs farther out through the gate.* SHE, *fallen at the side of the Altar burning, her head bowed, both hands conceal her face, feathers fly, green lights are strong, Altar burning,* WHITE BIRD *laughs from the Dome.* SHE WHO IS *Clara who is the Bastard who is the Virgin Mary suddenly looks like an owl, and lifts her bowed head, stares into space and speaks:) Ow . . . oww.* (FATHER *rises and slowly blows out candles on bed.)*

CURTAIN

A LESSON
in DEAD
LANGUAGE

The scene is a classroom, bright. A great WHITE DOG—*the
teacher—is seated at a great dark desk. Seven girl*
PUPILS *are seated at ordinary school desks. They
wear white organdy dresses, white socks and black
shoes. The* PUPILS *move stiffly. When the* PUPILS
*write, they write with their arms on imaginary
tablets. There are three blackboards, stage front,
left and right.*

*The statues of Jesus, Joseph, Mary, two Wise Men and a
shepherd are on a ridge around the room. The
statues are highly colored, wooden, and larger than
the* PUPILS. *(The* WHITE DOG *also appears larger
than the* PUPILS.) *Three statues are situated at the
front of the classroom, one on each side, and one at
the rear of the classroom.*

The DOG *appears to be in a position of a dog begging;
great, stiff, white. The actress who plays this role
should be costumed as a dog from the waist up.*

The WHITE DOG *sits at the desk. Her speech is unaccom-*

Original production at Theater Genesis, 1970, directed by
Gaby Rodgers.

panied by any movement of the mouth, since she should be wearing what resembles a mask.
The PUPILS *are seated, backs to audience, facing the* WHITE DOG.

WHITE DOG. *(Woman's voice.)* Lesson I bleed.

(The PUPILS *write in unison with their arms on imaginary tablets. What they write they speak aloud.)*

PUPILS. *(Slowly, dully.)* I bleed.
WHITE DOG. The day the white dog died, I started to bleed. Blood came out of me.
PUPILS. Teacher, the white dog died, I started to bleed. The white dog died, I started to bleed. Where are the lemons? I am bleeding, Mother.

(They put down their imaginary pens, sit erect with folded hands.)

WHITE DOG. Now, will the one who killed the white dog please come forward from the senate? *(The* PUPILS *turn their heads mechanically at each other to see who will come forward; they then turn back to the teacher, erect.)* Will the one who killed the white dog please come forward . . . And Caesar too, the one who killed Caesar.

(A silence. No one moves. Then one PUPIL *raises her hand. The* WHITE DOG *nods recognition.)*

PUPIL. I bleed, Teacher. I bleed. I am bleeding, Mother.
WHITE DOG. *(Ignores the* PUPIL.*)* I said will the one

who killed the white dog please come forward . . . And Caesar, at the foot of Pompey's statue . . .

(A silence. A PUPIL *raises her hand.)*

PUPIL. I bleed, Teacher, I bleed. It started when my white dog died. It was a charming little white dog. He ran beside me in the sun when I played a game with lemons on the green grass. And it started when I became a woman. My mother says it is because I am a woman that I bleed. Why, Mother, why do I bleed?

(They raise their hands.)

PUPILS. *(In unison.)* My mother says it is because I am a woman that I bleed. Blood comes out of me.

(They giggle tensely. Then they fold their hands. Silence. The PUPILS *stare at the* WHITE DOG—*the* WHITE DOG *stares at the* PUPILS.*)*

WHITE DOG. Since we do not know the one that killed the sun, we will all be punished. We will all bleed, since we do not know the one, we will all be punished. *(The* PUPILS *stand in the aisle, backs to audience. Silence. They each have a great circle of blood on the back of their dresses. They go stiffly to the three boards, three* PUPILS *at one board, two* PUPILS *at the other two.)* Write one hundred times, "Who killed the white dog and why do I bleed? I killed the white dog and that is why I must bleed. And the lemons and the grass and the sun. It was at the Ides of March."

(They pick up great white chalk and write on the boards

"Who killed.")

PUPILS. I killed the white dog and that is why I must bleed for Caesar. Dear Caesar.

(They write "I killed." Then the PUPILS *turn and face the* TEACHER. *One* PUPIL *raises her hand. The* WHITE DOG *nods recognition.)*

PUPIL. He ran beside me and the sky was blue and so was Mary's robe.
PUPILS. *(In unison.)* This bleeding started when Jesus and Joseph and Mary, the two Wise Men, and my shepherd died, and now Caesar.

(The PUPILS *look up at the statues in the room. The statues are bright.)*

STATUES. *(Voices from offstage.)* It started when Jesus and Joseph, Mary, the two Wise Men and the shepherd died. I found their bodies in the yard of my house. One day they disappeared and I found their bodies in the yard of my house tumbled down.
PUPIL. *(Raises her hand.)* I played a game with lemons in the green grass. I bleed too, Caesar. Dear Caesar.
PUPILS. My mother says it is because I am a woman.
STATUES. *(Offstage voices again.)* That I found the bodies on the grass at the Capitol at the foot of Pompey's statue.
PUPIL. They were the friends of my childhood. I bleed too, Caesar.

(A silence. No one writes. The WHITE DOG *stares at the* PUPILS. *The* PUPILS *stare at the* WHITE DOG. *Then*

the WHITE DOG *stares at the empty desks.)*

WHITE DOG. Calpurnia dreamed. Dear Caesar, I bleed too. *(A silence. The* PUPILS *stare at the* WHITE DOG.) Calpurnia dreamed a pinnacle was tumbling down. *(Another silence. The* WHITE DOG *stares at the pupils.)* Calpurnia dreamed. I am bleeding, Mother. Does no one know where the lemons are? Since no one knows, then we will all bleed and continue to bleed.

(PUPILS return to their seats, turn and face the WHITE DOG. *We again see the greater circle of blood on their dresses. They stand silently, then sit and fold their hands. A silence. A* PUPIL *raises her hand. The* WHITE DOG *nods.)*

PUPIL. Does no one know where we played a game of lemons in the sunshine is? Is it in the senate?

(A silence. The PUPILS *stare at each other.)*

SAME PUPIL. Teacher, why does no one know who killed the white dog? Mother, why does no one know? Why doesn't Caesar know who the conspirators are? *(A silence. The* PUPILS *stare at each other. The* SAME PUPIL *raises her hand.)* Teacher, my mother is sending me to the Asylum if I don't stop talking about my white dog that died and my bleeding and Jesus and the game in the green grass. I asked her who made me bleed. The conspirators, she said.
PUPILS. *(In unison.)* Who?
SAME PUPIL. The conspirators. And she said everything soon bleeds away and dies. Caesar, too.
PUPILS. Everything. And now Caesar, too. Dear Mother.

(A silence. The WHITE DOG *stares at the* PUPILS.)*

WHITE DOG. Calpurnia dreamed a pinnacle was tumbling down.

(The PUPILS *stare at the* WHITE DOG; *they fold their hands. Suddenly the* WHITE DOG *raps on the desk. The* WHITE DOG *rises, dims the room [imaginary light], stands in front of her desk.)*

PUPILS. *(Loud whispering.)* Calpurnia dreamed . . . *(Loud rapid whispering. The whispering stops. The* WHITE DOG *starts to walk through the aisles.)* Dear Caesar played a game of lemons in the sun on the green grass and my white dog ran beside. Jesus and Joseph and Mary, two Wise Men and the shepherd were friends of my childhood. Dear Mother.

(They look up at the statues. They put their heads down. The WHITE DOG *walks and comes to the end of the aisle; stands before the desk. A silence. Heads down. Another long silence.)*

WHITE DOG. Calpurnia dreamed.
PUPILS. *(Suddenly lift their heads and say:)* I bleed. I bleed. Ever since I became a woman. I bleed. Like Caesar will I bleed away and die? Since I became a woman blood comes out of me. I am a pinnacle tumbled down.

(Silence. They stand slowly. Their skirts are covered with blood. They stare at the WHITE DOG, *who stares at them. They hang their heads wearily. The stage becomes darker. Then a light comes slowly and fixes on a pupil to the right, rear, a pupil wearing a*

school dress. Her back is to us, her hands folded. Then a light to the WHITE DOG, *who turns slowly about a full circle, revealing a blank human face. She holds a great Latin book. The statues are revealed as statues of Romans. Pupils still stand, skirts covered with bright blood, heads hung. A silence. A bright light.)*

WHITE DOG. And what is the answer? Translate what I read.

(A silence. The PUPIL *raises her hand. The* WHITE DOG *nods recognition. A long pause.)*

PUPIL. *(Very slowly, as if translating.)* Calpurnia dreamed a pinnacle was tumbling down.

BLACKOUT

A RAT'S MASS

Characters:

> ROSEMARY
> BROTHER RAT
> SISTER RAT
> JESUS, JOSEPH, MARY, TWO WISE MEN,
> SHEPHERD

BROTHER RAT *has a rat's head, a human body, a tail.* SISTER RAT *has a rat's belly, a human head, a tail.* ROSEMARY *wears a Holy Communion dress and has worms in her hair. Mass said in prayer voices that later turn to gnawing voices. They were two pale Negro children.*

SCENE: *The rat's house. The house consists of a red carpet runner and candles. The light is the light of the end of a summer day.*
BROTHER RAT *is kneeling facing the audience.*

Original production by Ann and Carlton Colcord, New American Theatre, Rome, Italy, 1966, directed by Ben Ardery.

At the far left of the house stands a procession of JESUS, JOSEPH, MARY, TWO WISE MEN, *and a* SHEPHERD. SISTER RAT *stands at the end of the red aisle.*

BROTHER RAT. Kay within our room I see our dying baby, Nazis, screaming girls and cursing boys, empty swings, a dark sun. There are worms in the attic beams. *(Stands.)* They scream and say we are damned. I see dying and grey cats walking. Rosemary is atop the slide. Exalted! *(Kneels again.)* Kay within our room I see a dying baby, Nazis, again they scream. *(Stands again.)* and say we are damned. Within our once Capitol I see us dying. Rosemary is atop the slide exalted.

SISTER RAT. We swore on Rosemary's Holy Communion book.

BROTHER RAT. Did you tell? Does anyone know?

(The procession watches.)

SISTER RAT. Blake, we swore on our father's Bible the next day in the attic.

BROTHER RAT. Did you tell Sister Rat, does anyone know? *(Kneels.)* It was Easter and my fear of holy days, it was because it was Easter I made us swear.

SISTER RAT. Brother Rat, it was not Easter. It was night after Memorial Day.

BROTHER RAT. No, it was not after Memorial Day. It was the beginning of winter. Bombs fell. It was the War.

SISTER RAT. It was the War.

BROTHER RAT. Our fathers said everything was getting hung and shot in Europe. America wouldn't be safe long. *(Remains kneeling; procession marches across the house to center.)*

SISTER RAT. Remember . . . we lived in a Holy

Chapel with parents and Jesus, Joseph, Mary, our Wise Men and our Shepherd. People said we were the holiest children. *(*BROTHER RAT *turns face front.* SISTER RAT *comes down the aisle. Procession is still.* SISTER RAT *walking.)* Blake, our parents send me to Georgia. It is a house with people who say they are relatives and a garden of great sunflowers. Be my brother's keeper, Blake. I hide under the house, my rat's belly growing all day long I eat sunflower petals, I sit in the garden Blake and hang three gray cats. *(Stands before* BROTHER RAT.*)* Blake, I'm going to have a baby. I got our baby on the slide. *(Falls.)* Gray cats walk this house all summer I bury my face in the sand so I cannot bear the rats that hide in our attic beams. Blake, why did the War start? I want to hang myself.

BROTHER RAT. Kay, stop sending me the petals from Georgia. Stop saying our mother says you have to go to the State Hospital because of your breakdown. Stop saying you have a rat's belly.

(Procession marches across sound of rats.)

BROTHER AND SISTER RAT. The Nazis! *(Marching.)* The Nazis have invaded our house. *(Softer.)* Why did the War start? We want to hang ourselves. The rats. *(Sound.)* The rats have invaded our Cathedral. *(They rapidly light more candles. Procession returns, marches to the center.)* Our old Rosemary songs. Weren't they beautiful! Our Rosemary Mass. *(Procession watches; silence.)* Yet we weren't safe long. *(They look at Procession.)* Soon we will be getting shot and hung. Within our house is a giant slide. Brother and Sister Rat we are.

SISTER RAT. Blake, remember when we lived in our house with Jesus and Joseph and Mary?

BROTHER RAT. Now there are rats in the church

books behind every face in the congregation. They all have been on the slide. Every sister bleeds and every brother has made her bleed. The Communion wine.

BROTHER AND SISTER RAT. The Communion wine. Our father gives out the Communion wine and it turns to blood, a red aisle of blood. Too something is inside the altar listening. (SISTER RAT *kneels.*) When we were children we lived in our house, our mother blessed us greatly and God blessed us. Now they listen from the rat beams. *(Sound rats. They remain kneeling. Sound rats.)* It is our mother.

Rosemary, Rosemary was the first girl we ever fell in love with. She lived next door behind a grape arbor her father had built. She often told us stories of Italy and read to us from her Holy Catechism book. She was the prettiest girl in our school. It is one of those midwestern neighborhoods, Italians, Negroes and Jews. Rosemary always went to Catechism and wore Holy Communion dresses.

BROTHER RAT. Where are you going Rosemary? we say. And she says, "I have to go to Catechism." Why do you always go to Catechism? "Because I am Catholic"; then thinking, she says, "Colored people are not Catholics, are they?"

SISTER RAT. I don't think many.

BROTHER RAT. "Well I am. I am a descendant of the Pope and Julius Caesar and the Virgin Mary." Julius Caesar? "Yes, Caesar was the Emperor of all Italia." And are you his descendant? "Yes," she said.

BROTHER AND SISTER RAT. We wish we were descendants of this Caesar, we said, how holy you are, how holy and beautiful. She smiled.

BROTHER RAT. Our school had a picnic in the country and she took my hand. We walked to a place of white birch trees. It is our Palatine, she said. We are sailing to Italy, I said. She was the prettiest girl—the only thing, she has worms in her hair.

SISTER RAT. Great Caesars my brother and I were. Behold us singing greatly walking across our Palatine, my brother holding my hand and I holding his and we are young before the War O Italia. Rosemary was our best friend and taught us Latin and told us stories of Italy. O Rosemary songs.

BROTHER AND SISTER RAT. My sister and I when we were young before the War, and Rosemary our best friend, O Rosemary songs. Now we live in Rat's Chapel. My sister and I.

(BROTHER RAT *stares down the aisle.*)

BROTHER RAT. It is Rosemary. *(Stares.)* Did you tell? Does anyone know? Did you tell? Does anyone know? You started to cry Kay and I struck you in the face with our father's rifle. It was the beginning of summer. Just getting dark, we were playing and Rosemary said let's go to the playground. After you lay down on the slide so innocently Rosemary said if I loved her I would do what she said. Oh Kay. After that our hiding in the attic rats in the beam. Now there is snow on the playground, ambulances are on every street and within every ambulance is you Kay going to the hospital with a breakdown.

SISTER RAT. Blake, perhaps God will marry us in the State Hospital. Our fellow rats will attend us. Every day I look under our house to see who is listening. *(Aisle bright. Procession marches out.)* I cry all the time now . . . not sobbing . . . Blake, did we really go on that slide together? What were those things made us do while she watched?

BROTHER RAT. We hide in the attic like rats.

SISTER RAT. I cry all the time now.

BROTHER RAT. Within every ambulance is you,

Kay. Sister, all the time.

SISTER RAT. *(Sound rats.)* I am waiting for you Blake under the hospital so the Nazis won't see me.

(Procession marches to center.)

BROTHER RAT. The rat comes to the attic crying softly with her head down. She thinks she's going to have a baby. If I were a Nazi I'd shoot her. On the slide she said, Blake I am bleeding. Now there is blood on the aisle of our church. Before rat blood came onto the slide we sailed. We did not swing in chains before blood, we sang with Rosemary. Now I must go to battle. *(Heil. Salutes procession.)* Will you wait for me again at last spring? *(Procession does not answer.* BROTHER *and* SISTER RAT *fall down and light candles.* BROTHER RAT *stands. Stares down aisle.)* Will they wait for me at last spring Rosemary?

*(*ROSEMARY *comes down red aisle in her Holy Communion dress.)*

ROSEMARY. Blake the Nazis will get you on the battlefield.

*(*ROSEMARY *and* BROTHER RAT *stand before each other.* SISTER *remains kneeling.)*

BROTHER RAT. Rosemary atone us, take us beyond the Nazis. We must sail to the Capitol. Atone us. Deliver us unto your descendants.

ROSEMARY. The Nazis are going to get you.

BROTHER RAT. If you do not atone us Kay and I will die. We shall have to die to forget how every day this winter gray cats swing with sunflowers in their mouths because my sister thinks I am the father of a baby. Rosemary will you not atone us?

ROSEMARY. I will never atone you. Perhaps you can put a bullet in your head with your father's shotgun, then your holy battle will be done.

(The procession is at the edge of the house.)

SISTER RAT. *(Kneeling.)* O Holy Music return.

(The procession marches to center.)

ROSEMARY. Come with me, Blake.

BROTHER RAT. How can I ever reach last spring again if I come with you, Rosemary? I must forget how every day this winter gray cats swing with sunflowers in their mouths.

ROSEMARY. Perhaps you can put a bullet in your head.

SISTER RAT. I have a rat's belly.

BROTHER RAT. How can I ever again reach last spring if I come with you, Rosemary?

ROSEMARY. You must damn last spring in your heart. You will never see last spring again.

BROTHER AND SISTER RAT. Then we must put a bullet in our heads.

(Procession marches out. Silence. They stare at ROSEMARY. *Procession returns.)*

PROCESSION. Goodbye Kay and Blake. We are leaving you.

BROTHER AND SISTER RAT. Jesus, Joseph, Mary, Wise Men and Shepherd, do not leave. Great Caesars, we will be again, you will behold us as we were before Rosemary with the worms in her hair, a spring can come after the War.

PROCESSION. What Kay and Blake?

BROTHER AND SISTER RAT. A spring can come after the War when we grow up we will hang you so that we can run again, walk in the white birch trees. Jesus, Joseph, Wise Men, Shepherd, do not leave us.

PROCESSION. We are leaving because it was Easter.

BROTHER RAT. No, no, it was not Easter, it was the beginning of June.

PROCESSION. In our minds it was Easter. Goodbye Kay and Blake. *(They walk out. A gnawing sound. SISTER RAT kneels, BROTHER RAT and ROSEMARY face each other. A gnawing sound.)*

ROSEMARY. In my mind was a vision of us rats all.

BROTHER RAT. If only we could go back to our childhood.

SISTER RAT. Now there will always be rat blood on the rat walls of our rat house just like the blood that came onto the slide.

BROTHER RAT. Beyond my rat head there must remain a new Capitol where Great Kay and I will sing. But no within my shot head I see the dying baby Nazis and Georgia relatives screaming girls cursing boys a dark sun and my grave. I am damned. No . . . when I grow up I will swing again in white trees because beyond this dark rat run and gnawed petals there will remain a Capitol.

SISTER RAT. A Cathedral.

BROTHER RAT. Now within my mind I forever see dying rats. And gray cats walking. Rosemary worms in her hair atop the slide. Our Holy songs in our parents' house weren't they beautiful.

BROTHER AND SISTER RAT. Now it is our rat's mass.

(From now on their voices sound more like gnaws.) She said if you love me you will. It seemed so innocent. She said it was like a wedding. Now my sister Kay sends me gnawed petals from sunflowers at the State Hospital. She puts them in gray envelopes. Alone I go out to school and the movies. No more do I call by for Rosemary. She made me promise never to tell if you love me she screamed you'll never tell. And I do love her. I found my father's rifle in the attic. Winter time . . . gray time dark boys come laughing starting a game of horseshoes gnawing in the beams. The winter is a place of great gnawed sunflowers. I see them in every street in every room of our house. I pick up gnawed great yellow petals and pray to be atoned.

BROTHER RAT. I am praying to be atoned. I am praying to be atoned dear God. I am begging dear God to be atoned for the Holy Communion that existed between my sister and me and the love that I have for Rosemary. I am praying to be atoned. *(He kisses* ROSEMARY. *He comes down aisle, movements more rat-like . . . voice more like gnawing.)* Bombs fall I am alone in our old house with an attic full of dead rat babies. I must hide.

BROTHER AND SISTER RAT. God we ask you to stop throwing dead rat babies.

*(*BROTHER RAT *kneels.)*

BROTHER RAT. When I asked you yesterday the day they brought my sister Kay home from the State Hospital, you said God, Blake perhaps you must put a bullet in your head then your battle will be done. God, I think of Rosemary all the time. I love her. I told myself afterward it was one of the boys playing horseshoes who had done those horrible things on the slide with my sister. Yet I told Kay I am her keeper yet I told Rosemary I love her. It is the secret of my battlefield.

SISTER RAT. Here we are again in our attic where we once played games, but neither of us liked it because from time to time you could hear the rats. But it was our place to be alone, Blake now that I am home from the hospital we must rid our minds of my rat's belly. Can you see it? You did not visit me in the hospital Brother Rat. Blake I thought you were my brother's keeper.

BROTHER RAT. Everywhere I go I step in your blood. Rosemary I wanted you to love me. *(He turns— aisles bright—gnawing sound—battlefield sounds.)*

BROTHER AND SISTER RAT. God is hanging and shooting us.

SISTER RAT. Remember Brother Rat before I bled, before descending bombs and death on our capitol we walked the Palatine . . . we went to the movies. Now the Germans and Caesar's army are after us, Blake.

(He goes back to ROSEMARY *whose back is to him and starts.)*

ROSEMARY. The Nazis are after you. My greatest grief was your life together. My greatest grief.

BROTHER AND SISTER RAT. *(Look up.)* Now every time we will go outside we will walk over the grave of our dead baby Red aisle runners will be on the street when we come to the playground Rosemary will forever be atop the slide exalted with worms in her hair. *(They kneel then rise, kneel, then rise.)* We must very soon get rid of our rat heads so dying baby voices on the beams will no more say we are our lost Caesars.

ROSEMARY. It is our wedding now, Blake.

BROTHER AND SISTER RAT. Brother and Sister Rat we are very soon we must.

SISTER RAT. We are rats in the beam now.

ROSEMARY. My greatest grief was your life together. The Nazis will come soon now.

BROTHER AND SISTER RAT. Every time we go out red blood runners will be on the street. *(They kneel, then rise, kneel, then rise.)* At least soon very soon we will get rid of our rat heads and rat voices in beams will say no more we are your lost Caesars.

ROSEMARY. It is our wedding, Blake. The Nazis have come *(Marching.)* Brother and sister Rat you are now soon you will become headless and all will cease the dark sun will be bright no more and no more sounds of shooting in the distance. *(Marching procession appears bearing shotguns.)*

BROTHER AND SISTER RAT. We will become headless and all will cease the dark sun will be bright no more and no more sounds of shooting in the distance. It will be the end. *(The procession shoots, they scamper, more shots, they fall, ROSEMARY remains.)*

CURTAIN

SUN

Dedicated to Malcolm X

NOTE: MOVEMENTS

    Movements of the Man
    His orbiting
    Sun's orbiting
    Movements of the Moon
    Movements of the Sun
    Wire
    Revolving of the head

    MAN. Flowers and Water

Steel wire appears encircling them.

The adoration of kings and a
kneeling youth

Red flashes.

A madonna and a child, a man

Commissioned by the Royal Court Theatre, London, 1968.

A madonna and a child, a man
a madonna and a child and a
unicorn a study of a kneeling angel

(Red sun flashes top left. Moon image moves. MAN *watches
the red sun, tries to move his arms upward toward
it.)*

there exist landscapes flowers
and water views of the coast of
Italy cloudbursts lilies a
mountain a mountain of lilies

(A purple light. MAN *tries to move his arms.)*

and the heart,

(Red sun revolves. HE *watches it and tries to move. A yellow
light. Half of the Moon vanishes.* HE *watches it
fearfully over his shoulder as the half slowly drifts
away. Then before him* HE *watches red sun revolving. It disappears in front of him, lower left.* MAN *is
still, then looks again at vanished half moon.)*

Yes, and the heart and the tendrons
of the neck a landscape with a
view over a valley mountains
beyond a drawing of a square castle

(Orange sun appears top right. Greater hope.)

Yes, my heart and tendrons
of the neck landscapes mountains
a drawing of a square castle

(Moon still in half. Orange sun spins. MAN *watches greatly fearful as if the spinning sun held a grim omen, but goes on speaking hopefully.)*

the head of a man, yes a man's
head a man's shoulders the
organs of a woman an embryo
in the uterus the heart a
nude man a nude man
with his arms stretched out

(Pause. Intently watches orange sun spin.)

As a young man I felt myself
to be in the midst of sun

(Orange sun spins. Yellow sun now appears, spins. Beautiful sound. Could be this spinning.)

I liked to think my heart
led to light. Yet I discerned
coming dishonor.

(Sound and yellow and orange suns vanish. As always, when things vanish, MAN *is greatly perturbed. A black sun flashes top center then goes downward.* HE *watches its downward descent. Silence. Behind him the moon loses a quarter.* HE *watches it over his shoulder. The quarter vanishes slowly, moving away from him.)*

Yes the position of my blood vessels
the blood vessels in my face
a nude man with his arms

stretched out my lungs my
main arteries. *(Pause.)*
a branch of blackberry

(Black sun that has remained grows larger, a purple light.
MAN watches black sun grow large.)

Yes, water in motion a
spray of a plant a domed
church, a flying machine
horses horses and riders

(A yellow sun flashes orbits the wire vanishes. Moon still at
quarter. Now at lower right the MAN's disembodied
head appears. Large black sun vanishes wire starts
to move slowly in a circle. Long silence. MAN
speaks looking at dismembered head before him.)

My head, the head of Christ
the head of an apostle head
of St. Anne Head of the Virgin
Head of the infant St. John
Head of the infant Jesus. *(Pause.)*
my head dismembered

(Staring at his dismembered head disbelieving.)

No, I still dream children
children, the body and arms
of a child. *(Pause.)*
Yet my head. Dead

(HE goes on staring at his head as a black sun orbits twice.
New light comes onto the whole scene. Full moon

comes again, but a slightly different texture, more disturbing. Wire still slowly moving. MAN waits. The position of the moon, MAN, wire, head and all slightly change position so now less symmetry exists. The expression on the face of the head changes. All of these changes seem to be felt within the MAN since they are his inner state. The MAN'S own head grows distorted as HE watches the wire move around him. His head watches him, comes closer, smiles. Wire closer. Then a long waiting. Great imbalance of objects. Then loudly the moon fragments slowly and completely to pieces. Long fragmentation. HE tries to watch from his angular position. HE waits. Long fragmentation. Red sun appears top right. As the moon loudly totally framents behind him HE looks up at the new red sun.)

When a new sun appears
I think before I was born
my mother dreamed she saw
me in the sun then the
sun went down and at
night I appear within
the moon . . . And as the moon
fragments and all is imbalanced
I keep on thinking landscapes
flowers and water views
of the coast of Italy
cloudbursts lilies, a
mountain of lilies the heart

(Moon fragments again. Red sun revolves closer to MAN'S face. Orange sun appears, drops across him, dis-

appears. Head watches MAN *as* MAN *watches all.*
Fragmented moon, red sun, vanished orange sun.)

Yet all is in imbalance
no I must think of
trees, a tree, a tree
no a tree, a tree.
Water in motion

(Red sun revolves rapidly, closer to his own face and starts to
spin mysteriously, before his face.)

No rocks and streams
and flowers and violas
and sketches of landscapes
a river with a canal
alongside and a castle
on a hill flower rushes

(His dismembered head vanishes.)

star of Bethlehem
and other plants . . .
a spray of brambles

(Sun passes through his face leaving a light before him. Loud
noise of the moon fragmenting on his ear.)

No rocks and streams
and flowers and violas
and sketches of landscapes
a river with a canal
alongside and a castle
on a hill

(Louder fragmenting.)

flowering rushes, a star
of Bethlehem and other
plants . . . a spray of brambles

(A smell of a spray of brambles fills the air. MAN'S *arms
appear more disjointed.* MAN *continues loudly
fragmenting, an orange spinning sun appears lower
left dismembered head appears top left and starts to
orbit wire still revolving slowly a disembodied arm
appears lower right.)*

the sun is now myself
dismembered in darkness
my blood my dismembered
self at sundown on the moon.

*(*HE *watches his arm. The sun slowly vanishes moving
upward beyond his vision.* HE *understands that his own
arms are growing more disjointed. Noises of spattering.
Suddenly blood starts to run out of the fragmented moon.
Smell of blood.* MAN *grows more disjointed while his head
orbits and while blood runs out of the dark fragmented
moon. Great smell of blood, noises of spattering as if the
blood were falling against his head.)*

No the head of this man
a man's head and shoulders
the organs of my woman
as embryo in the uterus
its heart
this nude man
this nude man with his

arms stretched out

(HE *tries to stretch his arms. Suddenly many suns explode over the* MAN. *More blood pours out of the fragmented moon. More suns explode. Wire revolves closer to his head. His dismembered head. Still orbiting. A disembodied leg appears, vanishes. In the third time suns explode over the whole scene very slowly blood stops pouring out of the fragmented moon. Very slowly suns stop exploding and very slowly the fragmented moon changes into the* MAN *very slowly limb by limb the limbs slightly bloodied. Very slowly. At the same time his head silently revolves and at the same time very slowly blood comes onto his own face and* HE *becomes blotted out by it.* HE *lowers his blotted head. Silence. Head revolves. His own head blotted blank by blood.*)

When I was young I did
dream myself to be in the
midst of suns now fragmented
in the moon I am the head
of a bear the paws of a
dog the paws of a wolf
heads of monsters, a dragon . . .
a lizard symbolizing this truth
Now where is my head the
head of Christ the head of
an apostle head of St. Anne
Head of the Virgin head of
the infant St. John, head
of the infant Jesus. Where?

(Silence. Revolving head stops. Orange spinning sun appears, lower right. MAN, *now more disjointed, with blotted head.)*

I still dream of a woman
wearing a bodice of interlaced
ribbons a young woman
the head of a girl a girl's
braided hair the human
figure in a circle, man
man carrying earth
As my head moves
dead as the bones
and tendrons of
my arms move dead I still dream
Still I dream of the heart

(The whole scene starts moving into imbalance.)

The position of the blood vessels
in the neck and the face

(Dark blue and purple suns appear, revolve.)

A crowned eagle standing on a globe

(The moon, the MAN, *the wire the head all moving to a new imbalance. Then limb by limb the* MAN'S *body becomes blotted by blood.)*

Yes the heart
the head and shoulder of a man
muscles of the face and arms
a nude man

organs of a woman
an embryo in the uterus
the heart
Tuscany
A tree

(The MAN'S *body becomes more blotted by blood while the
symmetry of the scene is lost. Disembodied legs
appear then vanish.)*

Arezzo
Borgho
San Sepulchro
Perugia
Chiusi and Siena

*(The whole scene moves violently. The boundaries of the
moon vanish. Black suns revolve. In the moon*
MAN'S *body falls apart.)*

Two trees on the
bank of a stream
I still dream

*(His body in the moon falls apart as the moon totally loses
boundaries and all parts of his body fly into space.)*

A river with a rope ferry.

*(Wire breaks. Flashing grey and black suns. Collision of
objects. Great collision, then the* MAN *who is
blotted out by blood becomes smaller and smaller.
Great collision of his flying limbs.* MAN *becomes
smaller and smaller and vanishes into a tiny red sun.)*

Vanished MAN'S *voice:*

The Arno

(MAN *has vanished into a tiny red sun. Red sun turns black.*)

Vanished MAN'S *voice:*

A river with a canal alongside.

*(Flying limbs become still, vanish. Wire vanishes. All
vanishes. Except tiny black sun.)*

Vanished MAN'S *voice:*

And a castle on a hill
flowering rushes.
I still

DARKNESS

A MOVIE STAR
HAS to STAR
in BLACK and WHITE

A Movie Star Has to Star in Black and White was done as a work in progress at the New York Shakespeare Festival in New York on November 5, 1976, with the following cast:

Wallace	*Frank Adu*
Marlon Brando	*Ray Barry*
Eddie	*Robert Christian*
Paul Henreid	*Richard Dow*
Hattie	*Gloria Foster*
Montgomery Clift	*C. S. Hayward*
Jean Peters/	
Columbia Pictures Lady	*Karen Ludwig*
Clara	*Robbie McCauley*
Bette Davis	*Avra Petrides*
Shelley Winters	*Ellin Ruskin*

Director: Joseph Chaikin
Lights: Beverly Emmons
Costumes: Kate Carmel
Music: Peter Golub

Original production by Joseph Papp, at The New York Shakespeare Festival, 1976, directed by Joseph Chaikin.

NOTES: *The movie music throughout is romantic.*

The ship, the deck, the railings and the dark boat can all be done with lights and silhouettes.

All the colors are shades of black and white.

These movie stars are romantic and moving, never camp or farcical, and the attitudes of the supporting players to the movie stars is deadly serious.

The movie music sometimes plays at intervals when Clara's thought is still.

Characters

Clara
"Leading Roles" are played by actors who look exactly like:
Bette Davis
Paul Henreid
Jean Peters
Marlon Brando
Montgomery Clift
Shelley Winters

(They all look exactly like their movie roles.)

Supporting roles by
the mother
the father
the husband

(They all look like photographs Clara keeps of them except when they're in the hospital.)

Dark stage. From darkness center appears the COLUMBIA
PICTURES LADY *in a bright light.*

COLUMBIA PICTURES LADY. Summer, New York,
1955. Summer, Ohio, 1963. The scenes are *Now Voyager,
Viva Zapata* and *A Place In The Sun.*
   The leading roles are played by Bette Davis, Paul
Henreid, Jean Peters, Marlon Brando, Montgomery Clift
and Shelley Winters. Supporting roles are played by the
mother, the father, the husband. A bit role is played by
Clara.
   Now Voyager takes place in the hospital lobby.
   Viva Zapata takes place in the brother's room.
   A Place In The Sun takes place in Clara's old room.
June 1963.
   My producer is Joel Steinberg. He looks different
from what I once thought, not at all like that picture in
Vogue. He was in *Vogue* with a group of people who were
going to do a musical about Socrates. In the photograph
Joel's hair looked dark and his skin smooth. In real life his
skin is blotched. Everyone says he drinks a lot.
   Lately I think often of killing myself. Eddie Jr. plays
outside in the playground. I'm very lonely . . . Met Lee
Strasberg: the members of the playwrights unit were
invited to watch his scene. Geraldine Page, Rip Torn and
Norman Mailer were there. . . . I wonder why I lie so much
to my mother about how I feel. . . . My father once said his
life has been nothing but a life of hypocrisy and that's why
his photograph smiled. While Eddie Jr. plays outside I read

Edith Wharton, a book on Egypt and Chinua Achebe. Leroi Jones, Ted Joans and Allen Ginsburg are reading in the Village. Eddie comes every evening right before dark. He wants to know if I'll go back to him for the sake of our son.

(She fades. At the back of the stage as in a distance a dim light goes on a large doorway in the hospital. Visible is the foot of the white hospital bed and a figure lying upon it. Movie music. CLARA stands at the doorway of the room. She is a Negro woman of thirty-three wearing a maternity dress. She does not enter the room but turns away and stands very still. Movie music.)

CLARA. *(Reflective; very still facing away from the room.)* My brother is the same . . . my father is coming . . . very depressed.

Before I left New York I got my typewriter from the pawnshop. I'm terribly tired, trying to do a page a day, yet my play is coming together.

Each day I wonder with what or with whom can I co-exist in a true union?

(She turns and stares into her brother's room. Scene fades out; then bright lights that convey an ocean liner in motion.)

SCENE I

Movie music. On the deck of the ocean liner from Now Voyager *are* BETTE DAVIS *and* PAUL HENREID. *They sit at a table slightly off stage center.* BETTE DAVIS *has on a large white summer hat and* PAUL HENREID *a dark summer suit. The light is romantic and glamorous. Beyond backstage left are deck chairs. It is bright sunlight on the deck.*

BETTE DAVIS. *(To Paul.)* June 1955.

When I have the baby I wonder will I turn into a river of blood and die? My mother almost died when I was born. I've always felt sad that I couldn't have been an angel of mercy to my father and mother and saved them from their torment.

I used to hope when I was a little girl that one day I would rise above them, an angel with glowing wings and cover them with peace. But I failed. When I came among them it seems to me I did not bring them peace . . . but made them more disconsolate. The crosses they bore always made me sad.

The one reality I wanted never came true . . . to be their angel of mercy to unite them. I keep remembering the time my mother threatened to kill my father with the shot gun. I keep remembering my father's going away to marry a girl who talked to willow trees.

(Onto the deck wander the MOTHER, *the* FATHER, *and the* HUSBAND. *They are Negroes. The parents are as they were when young in 1929 in Atlanta, Georgia. The* MOTHER *is small, pale and very beautiful. She has on a white summer dress and white shoes. The* FATHER *is small and dark skinned. He has on a Morehouse sweater, knickers and a cap. They both are emotional and nervous. In presence both are romanticized. The* HUSBAND *is twenty-eight and handsome. He is dressed as in the summer of 1955 wearing a seersucker suit from Kleins that cost thirteen dollars.)*

BETTE DAVIS. In the scrapbook that my father left is a picture of my mother in Savannah, Georgia in 1929.

MOTHER. *(Sitting down in a deck chair, takes a cigarette out of a beaded purse and smokes nervously. She speaks bitterly in a voice with a strong Georgia accent.)* In our Georgia town the white people lived on one side. It had pavement on the streets and sidewalks and mail was delivered. The Negroes lived on the other side and the roads were dirt and had no sidewalk and you had to go to the post office to pick up your mail. In the center of Main Street was a fountain and white people drank on one side and Negroes drank on the other.

When a Negro bought something in a store he couldn't try it on. A Negro couldn't sit down at the soda fountain in the drug store but had to take his drink out. In the movies at Montefore you had to go in the side and up the stairs and sit in the last four rows.

When you arrived on the train from Cincinnati the first thing you saw was the WHITE AND COLORED signs at the depot. White people had one waiting room and we Negroes had another. We sat in only two cars and white people had the rest of the train.

(She is facing PAUL HENREID and BETTE DAVIS. The FATHER and the HUSBAND sit in deck chairs that face the other side of the sea. The FATHER also smokes. He sits hunched over with his head down thinking. The HUSBAND takes on old test book out of a battered briefcase and starts to study. He looks exhausted and has dark circles under his eyes. His suit is worn.)

BETTE DAVIS. My father used to say John Hope Franklin, Du Bois and Benjamin Mays were fine men.

(Bright sunlight on FATHER *sitting on other side of deck.* FATHER *gets up and comes toward them . . . to* BETTE DAVIS.)*

FATHER. Cleveland is a place for opportunity, leadership, a progressive city, a place for education, a chance to come out of the back woods of Georgia. We Negro leaders dream of leading our people out of the wilderness.

(He passes her and goes along the deck whistling. Movie music. BETTE DAVIS *stands up looking after the* FATHER *. . . then distractedly to* PAUL HENREID.)*

BETTE DAVIS. *(Very passionate.)* I'd give anything in the world if I could just once talk to Jesus.

Sometimes he walks through my room but he doesn't stop long enough for us to talk . . . he has an aureole. *(Then to the* FATHER *who is almost out of sight on the deck whistling.)* Why did you marry the girl who talked to willow trees? *(To* PAUL HENREID.) He left us to marry a girl who talked to willow trees.

*(*FATHER *is whistling,* MOTHER *is smoking, then the* FATHER *vanishes into a door on deck.* BETTE DAVIS *walks down to railing.* PAUL HENREID *follows her.)*

BETTE DAVIS. June 1955.

My mother said when she was a girl in the summers she didn't like to go out. She'd sit in the house and help her grandmother iron or shell peas and sometimes she'd sit on the steps.

My father used to come and sit on the steps. He asked her for her first "date." They went for a walk up the road and had an ice cream at Miss Ida's Icecream Parlor and walked back down the road. She was fifteen.

My mother says that my father was one of the most well thought of boys in the town, Negro or white. And he was so friendly. He always had a friendly word for everybody.

He used to tell my mother his dreams how he was going to go up north. There was opportunity for Negroes up north and when he was finished at Morehouse he was going to get a job in someplace like New York.

And she said when she walked down the road with my father people were so friendly.

He organized a colored baseball team in Montefore and he was the Captain. And she used to go and watch him play baseball and everybody called him "Cap."

Seven more months and the baby.

Eddie and I don't talk too much these days.

Very often I try to be in bed by the time he comes home.

Most nights I'm wide awake until at least four. I wake up about eight and then I have a headache.

When I'm wide awake I see Jesus a lot.

My mother is giving us the money for the doctor bill. Eddie told her he will pay it back.

Also got a letter from her; it said I hope things work out for you both. And pray, pray sometimes. Love Mother.

We also got a letter from Eddie's mother. Eddie's brother had told her that Eddie and I were having some problems. In her letter which was enclosed in a card she said when Eddie's sister had visited us she noticed that Eddie and I don't go to church. She said we mustn't forget the Lord, because God takes care of everything . . . God gives us peace and no matter what problems Eddie and I were having if we trusted in Him God would help us. It was the only letter from Eddie's mother that I ever saved.

Even though the card was Hallmark.

July 1955.

Eddie doesn't seem like the same person since he came back from Korea. And now I'm pregnant again. When I lost the baby he was thousands of miles away. All that bleeding. I'll never forgive him. The Red Cross let him send me a telegram to say he was sorry. I can't believe we used to be so in love on the campus and park the car and kiss and kiss. Yet I was a virgin when we married. A virgin who was to bleed and bleed . . . when I was in the hospital all I had was a photograph of Eddie in GI clothes standing in a woods in Korea. *(Pause.)* Eddie and I went to the Thalia on 95th and Broadway. There's a film festival this summer. We saw *Double Indemnity, The Red Shoes* and *A Place In The Sun.* Next week *Viva Zapata* is coming. Afterwards we went to Reinzis on Macdougal Street and had Viennese coffee. We forced an enthusiasm we didn't feel. We took the subway back up to 116th Street and walked to Bencroft Hall. In the middle of the night I woke up and wrote in my diary.

(A bright light at hospital doorway. CLARA younger, fragile, anxious. Movie music. She leaves hospital doorway and comes onto the deck from the door her father entered. She wears maternity dress, white wedgies, her hair is straightened as in the fifties. She has a passive beauty and is totally preoccupied. She pays no attention to anyone, only writing in a notebook. Her movie stars speak for her. CLARA lets her movie stars star in her life. BETTE DAVIS and PAUL

HENREID *are at the railing. The* MOTHER *is smoking. The* HUSBAND *gets up and comes across the deck carrying his battered briefcase. He speaks to* CLARA *who looks away.* PAUL HENREID *goes on staring at the sea.)*

HUSBAND. Clara, please tell me everything the doctor said about the delivery and how many days you'll be in the hospital.

(Instead of CLARA, BETTE DAVIS *replies.* PAUL HENREID *is oblivious of him.)*

BETTE DAVIS. *(Very remote.)* I get very jealous of you Eddie. You're doing something with your life.

(He tries to kiss CLARA. *She moves away and walks along the deck and writes in notebook.)*

BETTE DAVIS. *(To Eddie.)* Eddie, do you think I have floating anxiety? You said everyone in Korea had floating anxiety. I think I might have it. *(Pause.)* Do you think I'm catatonic?
EDDIE. *(Staring at Clara.)* I'm late to class now. We'll talk when I come home. *(He leaves.)* When I get paid I'm going to take you to Birdland. Dizzy's coming back.

(Movie music.)

CLARA. July.
I can't sleep. My head always full of thoughts night and day. I feel so nervous. Sometimes I hardly hear what people are saying. I'm writing a lot of my play, I don't want to show it to anyone though. Suppose it's no good. *(Reads*

her play.)

They are dragging his body across the green his white hair hanging down. They are taking off his shoes and he is stiff. I must get into the chapel to see him. I must. He is my blood father. God, let me in to his burial. *(He grabs her down center. She, kneeling.)* I call God and the Owl answers. *(Softer.)* It haunts my Tower calling, its feathers are blowing against the cell wall, speckled in the garden on the fig tree, it comes, feathered, great hollow-eyed with yellow skin and yellow eyes, the flying bastard. From my Tower I keep calling and the only answer is the Owl, God. *(Pause. Stands.)* I am only yearning for our kingdom, God.

(Movie music.)

BETTE DAVIS. *(At railing.)* My father tried to commit suicide once when I was in High School. It was the afternoon he was presented an award by the Mayor of Cleveland at a banquet celebrating the completion of the New Settlement building. It had taken my father seven years to raise money for the New Settlement which was the center of Negro life in our community. He was given credit for being the one without whom it couldn't have been done. It was his biggest achievement.

I went upstairs and found him whistling in his room. I asked him what was wrong. I want to see my dead mama and papa he said, that's all I really live for is to see my mama and papa. I stared at him. As I was about to leave the room he said I've been waiting to jump off the roof of the Settlement for a long time. I just had to wait until it was completed . . . and he went on whistling.

He had tried to jump off the roof but had fallen on a scaffold.

(Movie music. The deck has grown dark except for the light

on BETTE DAVIS *and* PAUL HENREID *and* CLARA.)

CLARA. I loved the wedding night scene from *Viva Zapata* and the scene where the peasants met Zapata on the road and forced the soldiers to take the rope from his neck . . . when they shot Zapata at the end I cried.

(Deck darker. She walks along the deck and into door, leaving PAUL HENREID *and* BETTE DAVIS *at railing. She arrives at the hospital doorway, then enters her brother's room, standing at the foot of his bed. Her brother is in a coma.)*

CLARA. *(To her brother.)* Once I asked you romantically when you came back to the United States on a short leave, how do you like Europe Wally? You were silent. Finally you said, I get into a lot of fights with the Germans. You stared at me. And got up and went into the dining room to the dark sideboard and got a drink.

(Darkness. Movie music.)

SCENE II

Hospital room and Viva Zapata. *The hospital bed is now totally visible. In it lies Wally in a white gown. The light of the room is twilight on a summer evening. Clara's brother is handsome and in his late twenties. Beyond the bed is steel hospital apparatus. Clara stands by her brother's bedside. There is no real separation from the hospital room and* Viva Zapata *and the ship lights as there should have been none in* Now Voyager. *Simultaneously brighter lights come up stage center. Wedding night scene in* Viva Zapata. *Yet it is still the stateroom within the ship.*

Movie music. MARLON BRANDO *and* JEAN PETERS *are sitting on the bed. They are both dressed as in* Viva Zapata.

JEAN PETERS. *(To Brando.)* July 11.

I saw my father today. He's come from Georgia to see my brother. He lives in Savannah with his second wife. He seemed smaller and hunched over. When I was young he seemed energetic, speaking before civic groups and rallying people to give money to the Negro Settlement.

In the last years he seems introspective, petty and angry. Today he was wearing a white nylon sports shirt that looked slightly too big . . . his dark arms thin. He had on a little straw sport hat cocked slightly to the side.

We stood together in my brother's room. My father touched my brother's bare foot with his hand. My brother is in a coma. *(Silent.)*

Eddie and I were married downstairs in this house. My brother was best man. We went to Colorado, but soon after Eddie was sent to Korea. My mother has always said that she felt if she and my father hadn't been fighting so much maybe I wouldn't have lost the baby. After I lost the baby I stopped writing to Eddie and decided I wanted to get a divorce when he came back from Korea. He hadn't been at Columbia long before I got pregnant again with Eddie Jr.

(MARLON BRANDO *listens. They kiss tenderly. She stands up. She is bleeding. She falls back on her bed.* BRANDO *pulls a sheet out from under her. The sheets are black. Movie music.)*

JEAN PETERS. The doctor says I have to stay in bed when I'm not at the hospital.

(From now until the end MARLON BRANDO *continuously helps* JEAN PETERS *change sheets. He puts the black sheets on the floor around them.)*

CLARA. *(To her brother, at the same time.)* Wally, you just have to get well. I know you will, even though you do not move or speak.

(Sits down by his bedside watching him. Her MOTHER *enters. She is wearing a rose colored summer dress and small hat. The mother is in her fifties now. She sits down by her son's bedside and holds his hand. Silence in the room. The light of the room is constant twilight. They are in the constant dim twilight while* BRANDO *and* PETERS *star in a dazzling wedding night light. Mexican peasant wedding music, Zapata remains throughout compassionate, heroic, tender. While* CLARA *and her* MOTHER *talk* BRANDO *and* PETERS *sit on the bed, then enact the Zapata teach-me-to-read scene in which* BRANDO *asks* PETERS *to get him a book and teach him to read.)*

MOTHER. What did I do? What did I do?
CLARA. What do you mean?
MOTHER. I don't know what I did to make my children so unhappy.

*(*JEAN PETERS *gets book for* BRANDO.*)*

CLARA. I'm not unhappy mother.
MOTHER. Yes you are.
CLARA. I'm not unhappy. I'm very happy. I just want to be a writer. Please don't think I'm unhappy.

MOTHER. Your family's not together and you don't seem happy. *(They sit and read.)*

CLARA. I'm very happy mother. Very. I've just won an award and I'm going to have a play produced. I'm very happy.

(Silence. The mother straightens the sheet on her son's bed.)

MOTHER. When you grow up in boarding school like I did, the thing you dream of most is to see your children together with their families.

CLARA. Mother you mustn't think I'm unhappy because I am, I really am, very happy.

MOTHER. I just pray you'll soon get yourself together and make some decisions about your life. I pray for you every night. Shouldn't you go back to Eddie especially since you're pregnant?

(There are shadows of the ship's lights as if Now Voyager *is still in motion.)*

CLARA. Mother, Eddie doesn't understand me.

(Silence. Twilight dimmer, MOTHER *holds Wally's hand. Movie light bright on* JEAN PETERS *and* MARLON BRANDO.)*

JEAN PETERS. My brother Wally's still alive.

CLARA. *(To her diary.)* Wally was in an accident. A telegram from my mother. Your brother was in an automobile accident . . . has been unconscious since last night in St. Luke's hospital. Love, Mother.

JEAN PETERS. Depressed.

CLARA. Came to Cleveland. Eddie came to La

Guardia to bring me money for my plane ticket and to say he was sorry about Wally who was best man at our wedding. Eddie looks at me with such sadness. It fills me with hatred for him and myself.

(BRANDO *is at the window looking down on the peasants. Mexican wedding music.*)

JEAN PETERS. Very depressed, and afraid at night since Eddie and I separated. I try to write a page a day on another play. It's going to be called a Lesson In Dead Language. The main image is a girl in a white organdy dress covered with menstrual blood.

(CLARA *is writing in her diary. Her* MOTHER *sits holding Wally's hand,* BRANDO *stares out the window,* JEAN PETERS *sits on the bed.* Now Voyager *ship, shadows and light.*)

CLARA. It is twilight outside and very warm. The window faces a lawn, very green, with a fountain beyond. Wally does not speak or move. He is in a coma. (*Twilight dims.*)

It bothers me that Eddie had to give me money for the ticket to come home. I don't have any money of my own: the option from my play is gone and I don't know how I will be able to work and take care of Eddie Jr. Maybe Eddie and I should go back together.

(FATHER *enters the room, stands at the foot of his son's bed. He is in his fifties now and wears a white nylon sports shirt a little too big, his dark arms thin, baggy pants and a little straw sports hat cocked to the side. He has been drinking. The moment he enters the room the mother takes out a cigarette and starts to nervously smoke. They do not look at each other. He speaks to* CLARA, *then glances in the direction of the* MOTHER. *He then touches his son's bare feet. Wally is lying on his back, his hands to his sides.* CLARA *gets up and goes to the window.* BRANDO *comes back and sits on the bed next to* JEAN PETERS. *They all remain for a long while silent. Suddenly the* MOTHER *goes and throws herself into her daughter's arms and cries.)*

MOTHER. The doctor said he doesn't see how Wally has much of a chance of surviving: his brain is damaged.

(She clings to her daughter and cries. Simultaneously.)

JEAN PETERS. *(To* BRANDO.) I'm writing on my play. It's about a girl who turns into an Owl. Ow. *(Recites from her writings.)* He came to me in the outhouse, in the fig tree. He told me, You are an owl, I am your beginning. I call God and the Owl answers. It haunts my tower, calling.

(Silence. FATHER *slightly drunk goes toward his former wife and his daughter. The* MOTHER *runs out of the room into the lobby.)*

MOTHER. I did everything to make you happy and still you left me for another woman.

*(*CLARA *stares out of the window.* FATHER *follows the* MOTHER *into the lobby and stares at her.* JEAN PETERS *stands up. She is bleeding. She falls back on the bed.* MARLON BRANDO *pulls a sheet out from under her. The sheets are black. Movie music.)*

JEAN PETERS. The doctor says I have to stay in bed when I'm not at the hospital.

(From now until the end MARLON BRANDO *continuously helps* JEAN PETERS *change sheets. He puts the black sheets on the floor around them.)*

JEAN PETERS. This reminds me of when Eddie was in Korea and I had the miscarriage. For days there was blood on the sheets. Eddie's letters from Korea were about a green hill. He sent me photographs of himself. The Red Cross, the letter said, says I cannot call you and I cannot come.

For a soldier to come home there has to be a death in the family.

MOTHER. *(In the hallway she breaks down further.)* I have never wanted to go back to the south to live. I hate it. I suffered nothing but humiliation and why should I have gone back there?

FATHER. You ought to have gone back with me. It's what I wanted to do.

MOTHER. I never wanted to go back.

FATHER. You yellow bastard. You're a yellow bastard. That's why you didn't want to go back.

MOTHER. You black nigger.

JEAN PETERS. *(Reciting her play.)* I call God and the Owl answers, it haunts my tower, calling, its feathers are blowing against the cell wall, it comes feathered, great hollow-eyes . . . with yellow skin and yellow eyes, the flying bastard. From my tower I keep calling and the only answer is the Owl.

July 8 I got a telegram from my mother. It said your brother has been in an accident and has been unconscious

since last night in St. Luke's hospital. Love, Mother. I came home.
My brother is in a white gown on white sheets.

(The MOTHER *and the* FATHER *walk away from one another. A sudden bright light on the Hospital Lobby and on Wally's room.* CLARA *has come to the doorway and watches her parents.)*

MOTHER. *(To both her former husband and her daughter.)* I was asleep and the police called and told me Wally didn't feel well and would I please come down to the police station and pick him up. When I arrived at the police station they told me they had just taken him to the hospital because he felt worse and they would drive to the hospital. When I arrived here the doctor told me the truth: Wally's car had crashed into another car at an intersection and Wally had been thrown from the car, his body hitting a mail box and he was close to death.

(Darkness.)

SCENE III

JEAN PETERS *and* BRANDO *are still sitting in* Viva Zapata *but now there are photographs above the bed of* CLARA'S *parents when they were young, as they were in* Now Voyager. *Wally's room is dark. Lights of the ship from* Now Voyager.

JEAN PETERS. Wally is not expected to live. *(She tries to stand.)* He does not move. He is in a coma. *(Pause.)* There are so many memories in this house. The rooms besiege me.

My brother has been living here in his old room with my mother. He is separated from his wife and every night has been driving his car crazily around the street where she now lives. On one of these nights was when he had the accident.

(JEAN PETERS *and* BRANDO *stare at each other. A small dark boat from side opposite Wally's room. In it are* SHELLEY WINTERS *and* MONTGOMERY CLIFT. CLARA *sits behind* SHELLEY WINTERS *writing in her notebook.* MONTGOMERY CLIFT *is rowing. It is* A Place In The Sun. *Movie music.* BRANDO *and* JEAN PETERS *continue to change sheets.*)

CLARA. I am bleeding. When I'm not at the hospital I have to stay in bed. I am writing my poems. Eddie's come from New York to see my brother. My brother does not speak or move.

(MONTGOMERY CLIFT *silently rows dark boat across.* CLARA *has on a nightgown and looks as if she has been very sick, and heartbroken by her brother's accident.* MONTGOMERY CLIFT, *as was* HENREID *and* BRANDO, *is mute. If they did speak they would speak lines from their actual movies. As the boat comes across* BRANDO *and* PETERS *are still. Movie music.* EDDIE *comes in room with* JEAN PETERS *and* BRANDO. *He still has his textbook and briefcase.* SHELLEY WINTERS *sits opposite* MONTGOMERY CLIFT *as in* A Place In The Sun. CLARA *is writing in her notebook.*)

EDDIE. (*To* JEAN PETERS; *simultaneously* CLARA *is writing in her diary.*) Are you sure you want to go on with this?

JEAN PETERS. This?

EDDIE. You know what I mean, this obsession of yours?

JEAN PETERS. Obsession?

EDDIE. Yes, this obsession to be a writer?

JEAN PETERS. Of course I'm sure.

(BRANDO *is reading.* CLARA *from the boat.*)

CLARA. I think the Steinbergs have lost interest in my play. I got a letter from them that said they have to go to Italy and would be in touch when they came back.

EDDIE. I have enough money for us to live well with my teaching. We could all be so happy.

CLARA. *(From boat.)* Ever since I was twelve I have secretly dreamed of being a writer. Everyone says it's unrealistic for a Negro to want to write.

Eddie says I've become shy and secretive and I can't accept the passage of time, and that my diaries consume me and that my diaries make me a spectator watching my life like watching a black and white movie.

He thinks sometimes . . . to me my life is one of my black and white movies that I love so . . . with me playing a bit part.

EDDIE. *(To* JEAN PETERS *looking up at the photographs.)* I wonder about your obsession to write about your parents when they were young. You didn't know them. Your mother's not young, your father's not young and we are not that young couple who came to New York in 1955, yet all you ever say to me is Eddie you don't seem the same since you came back from Korea.

(EDDIE *leaves.* MONTGOMERY CLIFT *rows as* SHELLEY

WINTERS *speaks to him. Lights on* BRANDO *and* PETERS *start slowly to dim.)*

SHELLEY WINTERS. *(To* MONTGOMERY CLIFT.) A Sunday Rain . . . our next door neighbor drove me through the empty Sunday streets to see my brother. He's the same. My father came by the house last night for the first time since he left Cleveland and he and my mother got into a fight and my mother started laughing. She just kept saying see I can laugh ha ha nothing can hurt me anymore. Nothing you can ever do, Wallace, will ever hurt me again, no one can hurt me since my baby is lying out there in that Hospital and nobody knows whether he's going to live or die. And very loudly again she said ha ha and started walking in circles in her white shoes. My father said how goddamn crazy she was and they started pushing each other. I begged them to stop. My father looked about crazily.

I hate this house. But it was my money that helped make a down payment on it and I can come here anytime I want. I can come here and see my daughter and you can't stop me, he said.

CLARA. *(To diary.)* The last week in March I called up my mother and I told her that Eddie and I were getting a divorce and I wanted to come to Cleveland right away.

She said I'm coming up there.

When, I said. When?

It was four o'clock in the afternoon.

When can you come I said.

I'll take the train tonight. I'll call you from the station.

Should I come and meet you?

No, I'll call you from the station.

She called at 10:35 that morning. She said she would take a taxi. I went down to the courtyard and waited. When she got out of the taxi I will never forget the expression on her face. Her face had a hundred lines in it. I'd never seen her look so sad.

CLARA. *(Reciting her play.)* They said: I had lost my mind, read so much, buried myself in my books. They said I should stay and teach summer school. But I went. All the way to London. Out there in the black taxi my cold hands were colder than ever. No sooner than I left the taxi and passed down a gray walk through a dark gate and into a garden where there were black ravens on the grass, when I broke down. Oow . . . oww.

SHELLEY WINTERS. This morning my father came by again. He said Clara I want to talk to you. I want you to know my side. Now, your mother has always thought she was better than me. You know Mr. Harrison raised her like a white girl, and your mother, mark my word, thinks she's better than me. (It was then I could smell the whiskey on his breath . . . he had already taken a drink from the bottle in his suitcase.)

(She looks anxiously at MONTGOMERY CLIFT *trying to get him to listen.)*

CLARA. *(Reading from her notebook.)* He came to me in the outhouse, in the garden, in the fig tree. He told me you are an owl, ow, oww, I am your beginning, ow. You belong here with us owls in the fig tree, not to somebody that cooks for your Goddamn Father, oww, and I ran to the outhouse in the night crying oww. Bastard they say, the people in the town all say Bastard, but I — I belong to God and the owls, ow, and I sat in the fig tree. My Goddamn Father is the Richest White Man in the Town, but I belong to the owls.

(Putting down her notebook. Lights shift back to PETERS

and BRANDO *on the bed.)*

JEAN PETERS. When my brother was in the army in Germany, he was involved in a crime and was court-martialled. He won't talk about it. I went to visit him in the stockade.

It was in a Quonset hut in New Jersey.

His head was shaven and he didn't have on any shoes. He has a vein that runs down his forehead and large brown eyes. When he was in high school he was in All City track in the two-twenty dash. We all thought he was going to be a great athlete. His dream was the Olympics. After high school he went to several colleges and left them; Morehouse (where my father went), Ohio State (where I went), and Western Reserve. I'm a failure he said. I can't make it in those schools. I'm tired. He suddenly joined the army.

After Wally left the army he worked nights as an orderly in hospitals; he liked the mental wards. For a few years every fall he started to school but dropped out after a few months. He and his wife married right before he was sent to Germany. He met her at Western Reserve and she graduated cum laude while he was a prisoner in the stockade.

(Movie music. Dark boat with MONTGOMERY CLIFT *and* SHELLEY WINTERS *reappears from opposite side.* MONTGOMERY CLIFT *rows.* CLARA *is crying.)*

SHELLEY WINTERS AND CLARA. Eddie's come from New York because my brother might die. He did not speak again today and did not move. We don't really know his condition. All we know is that his brain is possibly badly damaged. He doesn't speak or move.

JEAN PETERS. I am bleeding.

(Lights suddenly dim on MARLON BRANDO *and* JEAN PETERS. *Quite suddenly* SHELLEY WINTERS *stands up and falls "into the water." She is in the water, only her head is visible, calling silently.* MONTGOMERY CLIFT *stares at her. She continues to call silently as for help, but* MONTGOMERY CLIFT *only stares at her. Movie music.* CLARA *starts to speak as* SHELLEY WINTERS *continues to cry silently for help.)*

CLARA. The doctor said today that my brother will live; he will be brain damaged and paralyzed.

After he told us, my mother cried in my arms outside the hospital. We were standing on the steps, and she shook so that I thought both of us were going to fall headlong down the steps.

*(*SHELLEY WINTERS *drowns. Light goes down on* MONTGOMERY CLIFT *as he stares at* SHELLEY WINTERS *drowning. Lights on* CLARA. *Movie music. Darkness. Brief dazzling image of* COLUMBIA PICTURES LADY.)*

END

ELECTRA
(Euripides)

(The scene is outside the peasant's cottage. It is night, a little before sunrise.)

CHORUS:
Our ancient city Argos. The river. Inachus.

It was here that King Agamemnon led his army forth and with ships of war set sail for Troy.

And having killed the King of Troy and sacked that noble city he returned here to Argos. And on our temple walls hung high his trophies.

Abroad he had had good fortune. But here in his own home he died by his wife Clytemnestra's treachery, and her lover Aegithus's murderous hand.

Now Agamemnon is dead.

Aegisthus is king now. And Clytemnestra is now his wife.

Commissioned and first produced by Juilliard School of Music, 1980, directed by Michael Kahn.

As for the children left behind . . .

. . . the son of Orestes, Aegisthus resolved to kill, but an old slave took him off to Phocis,

Electra stayed in Argos and when she was of age nobles from all Hellas came to beg her hand.

Aegisthus, fearing if her husband were a prince, her noble son could avenge him for Agamemnon's death, kept her at home and let no one marry her.

But then he feared she might bear a son in secret by a nobleman so he planned to kill her.

Clytemnestra stopped him: She feared the hatred her child's death would bring on her.

So Aegisthus plotted a final scheme: He promised to anyone who killed Orestes . . . now in exile . . . a reward in gold.

And gave Electra in marriage to a peasant.

(Enter ELECTRA *from the cottage with a bucket. She puts it down.)*

PEASANT:
Electra why do you rise at dawn. You are a princess. You must rest.

ELECTRA:
I must go to the spring for water. I know you don't expect it of me but it's only right that I do my share and work with all the strength I have for our life.

PEASANT:
Go then if you wish to the spring. I will work in the fields this
morning. As soon as it grows lighter I will take the oxen out,
and do some harrowing.

(Exit ELECTRA *and* PEASANT. *Enter* ORESTES *and* PYLADES.)

ORESTES:
Ha! Pylades you're the man I trust above all others. I've
shared your home. You're a true friend the only one who has
honored me in spite of the condition to which I have fallen.

Now I have come, sent by Apollo's oracle home to shed the
blood of those who shed my father's blood.
Last night I visited my father's grave, offered tears, a shorn
lock and killed a lamb.
And now instead of entering the city, I have come to the
border to secretly search for my sister who, I have heard, is
married and lives near.

I must see her and get her help in executing our revenge.

Look, the dawn is rising. Let us find a ploughman whom we
can ask whether Electra lives near by.

Wait, a slave come weeping along the road.
For the moment, let's keep out of sight.

ELECTRA: *(Weeping.)*
Agamemnon was my father.
My mother was Clytemnestra.
And I am known to the people of Argos.
As "poor" Electra. My life is unbearable and you
my father lie dead, Agamemnon killed by Aegisthus.

My brother, what city holds you in bondage?
Sad in my room I dream of you.

a del femo pja pol i tia sek ra ta
deizmio lipi meni sto do mati omu
se oni revo me.

My cry of despair
Father I call to you in the deep Earth.
Hear my lamentation which fills my days,
Pateramu Pateramu
Cruel the axe's edge that cut your flesh.
Cruel the cunning that awaited you when you finished your
journey from Troy and your wife welcomed you home not
with a crown but with a two edged sword.

CHORUS:
Electra our princess, we've come to visit you to tell you of
the festival the day after tomorrow. All the unmarried girls
are getting ready to walk in the procession to Hera's temple.
We want you to come.

ELECTRA:
I cannot come. Fine dresses and necklaces of gold my dear
friends, make my heart sadder. I could not bear the sight of
the girls of Argos dancing, nor would I want to dance with
them.
Besides, look at me my hair is uncared for, my dresses are
rags. My appearance would bring shame to Agamemnon's
memory.

CHORUS:
Electra do come. The goddess Hera may inspire you. We

will get for you a lovely gown and a golden necklace.
Do you expect ever to overcome your enemies if you spend
your time weeping instead of praying to the Gods.
Your day of happiness will come, not from weeping, but
from praying on these feast and festival days. Come.

ELECTRA:
But my friends I have prayed.
Year after year.
But no god hears.
I've prayed for the king who died.
I've prayed for the prince who lives
exiled in an unknown country.
Still I am banished from my ancestral palace while my
mother lies with Aegisthus in a bed stained with murder.
Fo nos.

(Suddenly ORESTES *and* PYLADES *approach accompanied
by attendants.)*

ELECTRA: *(Behind chorus.)*
min me az ji zis!

ORESTES:
Perimene. Akuse. I bring news of your brother Orestes.

ELECTRA:
Tu a del fumo?

ORESTES:
Yes.

ELECTRA:
Is he alive or dead?

ORESTES:
He is alive.

ELECTRA:
Alive. *(Overcome for a moment.)* In what land is he living?

ORESTES:
He goes from city to city but allowed to be a citizen of none.

ELECTRA:
Is he hungry?

ORESTES:
He is not hungry but like a refugee and powerless.

ELECTRA:
Did he send a message to me?

ORESTES:
He yearned to know if you were alive and what kind of life you are living.

ELECTRA:
I have been devastated by grief as you can see.

ORESTES:
Yes, as I weep to see.

ELECTRA:
I've shorn my hair like the victims of the Scythians to mark my grief.

ORESTES:
To mark your grief for Orestes and for your father's death.

ELECTRA:
They were and are still dearer to me than life itself.

ORESTES:
Your brother loves you in that same way.

ELECTRA:
I know he loves me wherever he is.

ORESTES:
Tell me Electra, why do you live so distant from Argos?

ELECTRA:
I was forced to come here when I married.
My husband is from Mycenae.

ORESTES:
And this is your house?

ELECTRA:
Yes.

ORESTES:
It is very poor.

ELECTRA:
My husband is poor but he has shown me great kindness,
even reverence. He has never come near my bed. To him I
am still the princess Electra.

ORESTES:
Perhaps he thinks Orestes may return still and avenge him.

ELECTRA:
I think not. I think he acts from his heart. He reveres my royal ancestry.

ORESTES:
That will make Orestes happy. And Clytemnestra, did she stand back and let this cruelty be committed against you.

ELECTRA:
My mother cares for Aegisthus and only for Aegisthus and he is the one she listens to.

ORESTES:
What made Aegisthus do this to you?

ELECTRA:
He did not want me to have noble sons who could avenge him.

ORESTES:
Then you are powerless.

ELECTRA:
Yes.

(Silence between them.)

ORESTES:
These women around us. Are they friends?

ELECTRA:
Yes. They are my trusted friends.

ORESTES:
And I can speak openly?

ELECTRA:
Yes.

ORESTES:
Well then suppose Orestes comes, do you think he could carry out his killing?

ELECTRA:
He would have to be strong, as our father's murderers were.

ORESTES:
And Electra, would you be willing to help Orestes kill your mother?

ELECTRA:
I would, with the same axe with which she killed my father.

ORESTES:
I will tell him then that you are steadfast.

ELECTRA:
When I have shed my mother's blood as payment for my father's death then I can die content.

ORESTES:
I know these are words Orestes would want to hear you speak if he could see you.

ELECTRA:
If I saw him I would not recognize him.

ORESTES:
No, you were both young when you were parted.

ELECTRA:
There's only one who would know Orestes now.

ORESTES:
You mean the old slave who stole him away and saved his life.

ELECTRA:
Yes, that old man was my father's tutor.

ORESTES:
Tell me, was your father given a grave near his noble kin.

ELECTRA:
His body lies now where it fell, thrown out of doors, and no one is allowed to touch it.

ORESTES:
Orestes also yearns to know of the wrongs committed against you these past years.

ELECTRA:
I do not want my brother to anguish unduly. It is enough to tell him that I live exiled here on the border of the city. I have friends but my grief is such that I live mostly in solitude with my husband. Meanwhile our mother lives surrounded by the spoils of Troy that my father brought home. And Aegisthus who killed him gets into my father's own chariot and rides back and forth swaggering, clasping in his bloody hand the very sceptre which my father carried when he led

Hellas to war. On my father's grave no wine was poured, no wreath of of myrtle laid, dishonored, bare, there it lies.

Aegisthus when he's drunk, I've heard, jumps on the grave and flings stones at my father's name inscribed there and shouts, Where is your son Orestes? Why does he not return to protect your tomb?

ELECTRA:
So dear stranger I beg of you, tell Orestes everything I have said. I speak for myself and for his father. Agamemnon brought death to the Trojan nation. Ask him can he not kill one man?

(Enter the peasant.)

PEASANT: *(Frightened for* ELECTRA.*)*
Strangers what do you want at our door?
Electra you should not let strangers
come so close to our door.

ORESTES:
We bring great news,
We would never harm the princess Electra.

ELECTRA:
These two men have brought me word of Orestes.

PEASANT:
Orestes?

ELECTRA:
Yes.

PEASANT:
Is Orestes still alive?

ELECTRA:
Yes he is still alive and he has sent them word of me.

PEASANT:
Is this true?

ORESTES:
On my honor I swear it.

ELECTRA: *(To men.)*
This is the man who is known as "poor Electra's husband."

PEASANT:
For this great news, please come inside. Such that we have is yours.

ORESTES:
Let us accept this house's hospitality.

(Exit ORESTES and PYLADES into the cottage.)

ELECTRA: *(To her husband.)*
You know how bare our house is. These two guests are far above our level. Why must you ask them in?

PEASANT:
Why not? If they're as noble as they look they'll be at home in this cottage.

ELECTRA:
Since you've done it now,

Go quickly and find my father's old servant, who since they turned him out of Argos, tends a flock of sheep close to the Spartan frontier.

Tell him we have guests and he must come and bring something that I can cook and give them. He'll be joyful to know my brother, the child he once saved, still lives. He'll bless the gods.

PEASANT:
I'll go now to the old man and take your message. You go in now and get things ready.

(Exit ELECTRA *and* PEASANT.*)*

CHORUS:
Long ago in the mountains of Argos,
A soft young lamb was found by Pan,

And the lamb had a lovely fleece of pure gold.
And Pan, they say, brought it to Atreus king of Argos.

And lovely songs rose loud
In praise of the golden lamb.

Then Thyestes lay secretly with Atreus' wife,
And persuaded her and took the marvelous lamb to his own house.

Then going forth to the assembled people he proclaimed
That he held in his own house
The lamb with the golden fleece.

Then it was that Zeus turned back
The glittering journeys of the stars,

And from that day on, the blaze of divine fire

Drives always toward the western sky;
And the parched plains of Ammon languish untouched by
dew.
And Zeus withholds from them his sweet rain.

That is the story.

But I can hardly believe

That the golden sun

Changed his burning course,

To requite a human sin.

Nevertheless,

frightening tales are useful:
They promote a reverence for the gods.

O Clytemnestra,

Had you but remembered tales like these
As you raised your hand to kill your husband.

(Enter OLD MAN *carrying flowers and a lamb.)*

      OLD MAN:
Electra my princess. Electra. *(*ELECTRA *appears at the
door.)* I've brought you a lamb bred in my own flock, took it

from the ewe this morning, flowers and cheese straight from the press. And here's some old rich-scented wine. Let someone take this into the strangers. For at this moment my eyes are full of tears.

ELECTRA:
Why are you weeping old man?

OLD MAN:
On my way here I passed your father's grave. I knelt and shed tears and then I opened this wineskin and poured wine as an offering,
When I saw there on the altar a black fleeced ewe just newly sacrificed, the blood still wet, and beside it a lock of hair. What man would dare visit that grave? No Argive would. Do you think your brother could have come here secretly and paid reverence to his father's desolate tomb? Electra go there. Match that hair with your very own, see if it is the same.

ELECTRA:
Even if it were Orestes' hair it would not match mine. Orestes' hair was grown like an athlete's in the palaestra and mine like a woman's softened by combing.
And besides, I do not think my brave Orestes would come to Argos secretly.

OLD MAN:
That may be true; but still, go and see if the size and shape of the footprints near the grave are like your own.

ELECTRA:
How could there be footprints on rocky ground?

No, either a stranger pitied the sad grave and laid the lock there or some Argive dared the guards and made these offerings.

OLD MAN:
Well, where are these strangers? I want to see them.

ELECTRA:
Here they come.

(Enter PYLADES *and* ORESTES.*)*

OLD MAN:
My greetings to you strangers.

ORESTES *and* PYLADES:
Greetings Old Man.

ORESTES:
Electra whose friend is this man's?

ELECTRA:
This man was my father's tutor.

ORESTES: *(Strangely.)*
The same man that got your brother safely away.

ELECTRA:
Orestes owes his life to him.

ORESTES:
Why does he stare at me? Perhaps he thinks I am like someone.

(The OLD MAN *stares at* ORESTES.)

OLD MAN:
Stranger, that scar on your brow. How did you come by it?

ORESTES:
I fell and cut it once.

OLD MAN:
You fell and cut it once when chasing a fawn.

ORESTES:
Yes I fell and cut it once when chasing a fawn.

OLD MAN:
You fell and cut it once when chasing a fawn with me.

ORESTES:
I fell and cut it once when chasing a fawn with you.

*(*ELECTRA *stares at them.)*

OLD MAN:
My princess look at this man before you.

ORESTES:
Yes, Princess Electra, look closely at this man before you.

OLD MAN:
Princess Electra it is your brother.
It is Orestes.

ELECTRA:
O my brother. Is it you?

ORESTES:
Yes. Electra.

(They run and embrace.)

ELECTRA:
I thought you'd never come. O res ti mo

ORESTES:
a ga pi me ni mu a del fi

ELECTRA:
I had despaired.

ORESTES:
I too.

ELECTRA:
You really are Orestes.

ORESTES:
Yes. Your one ally.
(To OLD MAN.*)* Now tell me old man, have I any friends in
Argos?
Or am I bankrupt . . . as in fortune . . . so in all?
Shall I go by night or day?
What way shall I set out to meet my enemies?

OLD MAN:
My son you are an exile: you have not one friend. In your old
friends' eyes you are finished; no one pins his hopes on you.

ORESTES:
I want to get back to Argos and my father's house.

OLD MAN:

If that's your aim then you must kill Aegisthus and your mother.

ORESTES:

That's the deed I've come for.

OLD MAN:

As I see it, it's useless to think of getting inside the walls of the royal house. Aegisthus has sentries everywhere. He's greatly fearful, it is rumored, and cannot sleep at night. But listen. Fortune may have intervened. On my way here I saw Aegisthus.

ORESTES:

Where? Pu je ron da

OLD MAN:

Not far away in the pastures where his horses graze.

ORESTES:

What was he doing?

OLD MAN:

Preparing a banquet for the Nymphs. He had everything in hand to sacrifice a bull.

ORESTES:

Were his men with him or had he just slaves?

OLD MAN:

Only his slaves were there. No Argives.

ORESTES:
Would there be some who would recognize me?

OLD MAN:
No. They're slaves recently come to Argos. They've never
seen you.

ORESTES:
I wonder how I can get close to him.

OLD MAN:
Perhaps you could just go and stand along the road near the
sacrifice so he will see you.

ORESTES:
And then.

OLD MAN:
Often he can't resist playing the role of King. He may
command you to join him.

ORESTES:
I will go at once. Once I am there I will make my plan. Was
my mother with him?

OLD MAN:
She is in Argos still. She is afraid to go too much among the
people. She is much hated.

ORESTES:
Then it will be difficult to kill both of them.
And they must die at the same time.

ELECTRA:
The killing of my mother I shall claim myself.

ORESTES:
Then we shall succeed.

ELECTRA:
Old Man will you help us?

OLD MAN:
I will. What plan do you have for Clytemnestra's death?

ELECTRA:
This: Go and tell her I have borne a child . . . a son. Say it was ten days ago.

OLD MAN:
And how will this bring about your mother's death?

ELECTRA:
When she is told of the birth of my son I know she will come.

OLD MAN:
And why would she come, she who has disgraced you so.

ELECTRA:
I know her well. She will come and pretend to weep over my son's lowly birth.

OLD MAN:
Perhaps. And then once here?

ELECTRA:
Once here, we will be ready.

OLD MAN:
If I see Clytemnestra's death then I can die content.

ELECTRA:
But first now you must show my brother where to go to find
Aegisthus. And then go to my mother and tell her what I
have said.

OLD MAN:
I will speak your very words.

ELECTRA:
Orestes. Our moment at last has come.

(They raise their hands in prayer.)

ORESTES:
Zeus. Help us conquer our father's enemies and ours.

ELECTRA:
And have pity on us for our days have been pitiable.

OLD MAN:
Send strength to these dear children.

ORESTES:
Bring the army of the dead to fight with us.

ELECTRA:
Bring the brave who shared the victory over Troy.

OLD MAN:
Bring all who hate impure hearts.

(Pause. ORESTES *and* OLD MAN *rise.)*

ELECTRA:
Father, can you hear?

OLD MAN:
He has heard all. I am certain. It is time to go.

*(*ELECTRA *rises.)*

ELECTRA:
Orestes I give you my unbroken word. If in the struggle you lose your life, be sure I shall not live. I'll drive a sword into my heart.

ORESTES:
I understand.

ELECTRA:
Then take your courage in both hands.

(Exit ORESTES, PYLADES, OLD MAN.*)*

(To women.) My friends, your part will be to be beacons and to raise the cry for life or death. I'll be on watch too holding this sword. If Orestes is defeated, our enemies shall not wreak vengeance on his sister. *(She exits.)*

*(*CHORUS *assumes lookout positions; a death cry is heard.)*

CHORUS:
What was that sound?
Electra, princess, come.

ELECTRA:
What is it?

CHORUS:
We heard a cry like death.

ELECTRA:
I heard the cry too.

CHORUS:
It comes from far off.

ELECTRA:
That was my brother. This means the sword for me now.

CHORUS:
Wait Electra, until we hear the cries once more.

ELECTRA:
We have lost. I fear it.

CHORUS:
Wait . . . here in the darkness comes a messenger.

(They face him.)

MESSENGER:
Victory, women of Mycenae, Victory.
I proclaim Orestes' Victory.

Aegisthus, Agamemnon's murderer lies dead.
Praise be to the gods.

ELECTRA:
di ke o si ni il thes epi tel lus
Tell me. Tell me of his death.

MESSENGER:
After we left this cottage we reached a road and we
followed this road to where Aegisthus was. He stood in a
field cutting young myrtle leaves to make a garland for his
head.
When he saw us he called out "Greetings Strangers. Where
do you come from?"
And Orestes said "We are from Thessaly. We are on our way
to Delphi to sacrifice to Zeus.
Then Aegisthus said, "Stay here, be my guests, I'm killing a
bull in honor of the nymphs and you must share the
banquet. I won't let you refuse.
"Slaves bring holy water for these guests. Come here to the
purifying bowl."

Orestes answered, "We purified ourselves down the road
there in holy water from a stream.
So Aegisthus, if strangers may join in the sacrifice with
Argive, we will not refuse you." The slaves guarding the
King lay down their spears, being busy lighting fires,
preparing the sacrificial bowl.

Then Aegisthus took barley and threw it on the altar.
"May evil suppress my enemies," he said, by which he
meant you and Orestes. Then he said to Orestes,
"I've heard it said that Men of Thessaly are expert at cutting
up a dead bull skillfully, friend, here's the sword.

Show us now if that's true."
It was a wellmade Dorian sword. Orestes grasped it firm
threw off his coat then took the bull-calf's leg
and with one stroke laid the bull's flesh bare,
severed the carcass then opened up the guts.
Aegisthus took augural parts and gazed at them.
The liver lobe was missing and the portal vein
and the gall bladder portended evil visitations.
The king's face grew dark.
Orestes said, "What has upset you?"
"Friend," replied Aegisthus, "I'm much in fear of treachery
from abroad. Agamemnon's son is the most dangerous
enemy to me and to my royal house."
Orestes said, "What you, a king, fear an exile's plots?
This Dorian knife's too small, bring me a Phythian sword.
I'll split the breast bone, and we can feast."
They brought one, and he cut bending over the augural
parts.
Orestes then rose and struck him on the joint of his neck
shattering his spine. His whole body writhed in agony and
death.
The King's guard now seized their spears. But Pylades and
Orestes stood their ground.
Orestes cried out, "I am Orestes. This man was my father's
murderer whom I have punished.
At this they withdrew. At that instant he was recognized by
an old man who had long served the royal house. "It is
Orestes" he said.
And suddenly they started to cheer and shout with delight.
They put garlands on him. Now he's coming here bringing
the body of Aegisthus.

CHORUS:
Oh, Electra, blood has paid for blood.

Set your feet dancing.
Dance like the light. *(Piano in.)*
O o res tis e ker vi se lam bri ko ro na
e la te na ho rep su me

ELECTRA:
o egistos kitete nekros ekinos
pu katastrepse tinzoi tu pateramu
Come friends.
My finery that I possess that is
stored in the cottage I will
bring out.
Too I will bring the crown
for my brother's head.

CHORUS:
Go Electra, bring the crown for Orestes.
While we dance to the muses.

*(Chant resumes under dance sequence. The dance comes to
an end when sight of the dead body of* AEGISTHUS
occurs.)

ELECTRA: *(Placing a crown on* ORESTES' *head and
then* PYLADES.)
El a adelfumu afiseme nastere oso
Sto ke falisu aftingorona
Iltes piso fernondas to dikeo
Pu mas a niki ke o eh trosmas
Vris kete pj a ne kros sta podia mas
je ne e mu niki ti
(To PYLADES.) Ke e si piladi
E pisis lave ap ta her jamu
Af to to niki ti rio stefani

ORESTES:
Do what you wish: throw out his carcass to the dogs. Impale him on a stake to feed the birds of heaven. He's yours Electra, once your master, now your slave.

ELECTRA: *(To the body.)*
You were the ruin of our life. My brother and I did you no harm but you made us fatherless.

ELECTRA:
Take his body and put it out of sight. My mother must not see it before her throat is cut.

(ORESTES *sees* CLYTEMNESTRA *approaching in the distance.)*

ORESTES:
Wait. There are other things we must decide.

ELECTRA:
What is it? *(Looking in the same direction.)*
An armed force from Mycenae.

ORESTES:
No it is our mother.

ELECTRA:
Good, she is stepping into the trap. Look how fine she is . . . A carriage, slaves, and her best gown.

ORESTES:
What shall we do then? Are we really going to kill our mother?

ELECTRA:
Have you grown soft as soon as you set eyes on her?

ORESTES:
She bore me, she brought me up, how can I take her life?

ELECTRA:
How? As she took our father's life.

ORESTES:
It is wrong to kill my mother!

ELECTRA:
You avenge your father.

ORESTES:
Avenging him I am pure; but killing her condemned.

ELECTRA:
If you neglect to avenge him you defy the gods.

ORESTES:
But if I kill my mother shall I not be punished?

ELECTRA:
He will pursue you if you let his vengeance go.

ORESTES:
Some monster disguised as a god has commanded me. But I can't believe what the god told me is right.

ELECTRA:
You cannot lose your nerve and be the coward now. You must use the same deception she used when with Aegisthus'

help she struck our father down.

ORESTES:
I'll go in. Every step is dreadful and the deed before me still more dreadful yet if heaven so wills, let it be done.

(*Exit* ORESTES *and* PYLADES *into the house; enter* CLYTEM-NESTRA *attended by female slaves.*)

CLYTEMNESTRA:
Set down the carriage, trojan slaves. Take my hand and help me to this place.

ELECTRA:
Will you give me the privilege to hold your royal hand mother? I too am a slave who you took prisoner by sword.

CLYTEMNESTRA:
Your father brought all this on you by wicked treachery. When I married I did not expect to see my children killed. He took my child to Aulis where the fleet lay bound, lured from home with lies about Achilles and cut her soft white throat. My Iphegenia. If he had done it to avert the capture of his city, or to exalt his house he could be forgiven but to sacrifice my child so that the fleet might have good winds that I cannot forgive. And that was Agamemnon's reason for murdering my daughter.
Even then as wicked as it was, I would not have turned savage or killed him. But he brought home with him the whore Cassandra and kept us both in one house. So I killed him. I took the only way open to me. I turned for help to his enemies. Well, what else could I do.

ELECTRA:
You destroyed the life of the most noble man in Hellas. You pretend that you avenge your daughter with my father's blood.
There may be some who believe you but I know you.
Before Iphigenia's sacrifice was decided on . . . when Agamemnon was scarcely out of sight you began seeking what you should not. If Troy lost a battle your eyes clouded. Why? Because you didn't want Agamemnon to come back to Argos. I saw the way you looked at Aegisthus. Even if as you say, our father killed Iphigenia, what did my brother and I do to you? After you killed our father you exiled us from our house and bought yourself a lover with your dowry.
So if death demands justice then Orestes must kill you.
If one revenge is just so is the other.

CLYTEMNESTRA:
Electra, I regret that revenge now.

ELECTRA:
It is too late for regret. But Orestes lives. Why do you not bring him home?

CLYTEMNESTRA:
I am frightened for myself. They say Orestes is mad with anger over his father's death.

ELECTRA:
And why do you let Aegisthus still persecute me?

(CLYTEMNESTRA *turns away. Silence.*)

CLYTEMNESTRA: *(Abruptly.)*
Why did you send for me?

ELECTRA:
You were told of my confinement were you not?

CLYTEMNESTRA:
I was. But why are you in this state, so ill-looking? The birth's well over now.

ELECTRA:
Will you do this for me? Offer the tenth day sacrifice for a son.

CLYTEMNESTRA:
It is usually done by the woman who delivered you.

ELECTRA:
I was alone. I delivered myself.

CLYTEMNESTRA:
What? In this house so far from any neighbor.

ELECTRA:
We are poor; we don't have friends.

CLYTEMNESTRA:
Well as a favor, I'll go in and pay the gods the respect for your son. And then I must go to where my husband's sacrificing to the nymphs out in the pasture. *(To servants.)* You there take the carriage away. And feed the horses. Give me as much time as I need to make this offering to the gods; then come for me. *(To* ELECTRA.) I have my husband to think of.

ELECTRA:
Please come in. (CLYTEMNESTRA *goes in.*) All is prepared.
The sword is sharpened for you. In the house of death you
shall still be his bride whose bed you shared in life.

*(*ELECTRA *goes in.)*

CHORUS:
Now retribution follows sin.
Through the fated house a new wind blows
Long ago my beloved Lord and King fell dead

Now retribution follows sin
Through the fated house a new wind blows
Long ago my beloved Lord and King fell dead

And through the rooms round the stone cornice
rang out his death cry.

O wicked wife why do you murder me,
returned after ten harvests
home to my country?

Now like a returning tide
justice comes to the reckless Clytemnestra.

CLYTEMNESTRA:
Ped ya mu ya to o no ma ton te on
mi n sko to ne te tim mi ter as as
vo i thia ach ach
Soon or late heaven dispenses justice
Her revenge on her husband was unholy

CHORUS:
Now Electra and Orestes come clothed

in fresh streams of their mother's blood.
Now Electra and Orestes come clothed
in fresh streams of their mother's blood.

i e lek tra ke o o re tis vu tij meni
sto fresko hye meno e: ma tis miterastus
(All together on last "miterastus." Enter ORESTES, ELECTRA,
and PYLADES *with body of* CLYTEMNESTRA.)

ORESTES:
o: yi o zef e si puv le pis o la osa i an
tro pi ka non ki tak se af to af to to e ma ti ro
te a ma di o so mata hti pi me na a paf to to hye ri

ELECTRA:
I am guilty too. I burned with desperate rage against her, yet
she was my mother. *(My mother in Greek repeated.)* i mi ter
amu

ORESTES:
O Apollo.
You have bestowed on me
a murderers destiny.
To what city shall I go.
Will any friend, will any man who fears god,
Dare to look into my face . . . a son who has killed his
mother?

ELECTRA:
O what shall we do? O: ti fa ka no me.
Where shall we go? pu Oa pa me
(Repeat in Greek.)

ORESTES:
Did you see how in her agony
she opened her gown, thrust forth her breast
and showed it to me as I struck.
The body that gave me birth sprawled on the ground.

ELECTRA:
As she uttered a shriek she put her hand on my face.
"My child I implore you" she said. Then she hung around
my neck so that the sword fell out of my hand.

ORESTES:
I held my cloak over my eyes
while with my sword I drove
the blade into my mother's throat.

ELECTRA:
I urged you on and held the sword, my hand beside yours.

ORESTES:
Come help me cover her limbs with her dress and close her
wounds.

ELECTRA:
As we wrap this cloak around her.
We loved you . . . although we hated you.

CHORUS:
This is the prophetic end of great sorrow.

CURTAIN

ORESTES
(Euripides)

(ELECTRA *enters; haunted looking and wan, watching over* ORESTES. *Voices enter, sustained chord.*)

CHORUS:
After the murder Orestes collapsed.
He lies in his bed seized by a raging fever.
And driven on to madness by his mother's ghost
and Eumenides who pursue him.

Six days since they sent her body to the pyre and six days he has not tasted food but lies there submerged in blankets.

Sometimes he madly rises from bed crying out. The Argives have forbidden anyone to speak to them or shelter them.

Today the Argives meet to decide whether they shall live or die and if they will die by stoning or the sword.

One single hope is left.
Their uncle Menelaus has come home from Troy. His fleet

Commissioned and first produced by Juilliard School of Music, 1980, directed by Michael Kahn.

fills the harbor at Nauplia. He has brought Helen.

She so fears being killed by the fathers of those who died at Troy that Menelaus sent her ahead last night in darkness. She is in the palace weeping over her sister's, their mother's, death.

She has one consolation, her daughter Hermione, whom as a child she entrusted to their mother's care.

She has some comfort left but they do not so they sit watching the road in hope that Menelaus will come. Unless he helps them, they must die.

(Enter HELEN, *not young but vain of her beauty. She carries a pitcher for libations and small locks of her hair.)*

 HELEN: *(To herself.)*
Poor Clytemnestra. And to think I sailed for Troy without seeing her. Some god must have made me mad. *(Looking at* ORESTES.) When did he fall into this state?

 ELECTRA:
The day we spilt our mother's blood.

 HELEN: *(Turning abruptly from* ORESTES.)
I want you to help me Electra. I want you to go to my sister's grave.

 ELECTRA:
What? You want me to go to my mother's grave? But why?

 HELEN:
To pour libations on her grave and leave these shorn strands

of my hair.

ELECTRA:
But my mother was your sister. You go yourself.

HELEN:
I am afraid.
I am afraid of the fathers of the soldiers who died at Troy.
Please go.
I do not want to walk the streets of Argos.
I am despised by the women here.

ELECTRA:
No. I cannot bear the sight of my mother's grave.

HELEN:
What can I do? I cannot send a servant.

ELECTRA:
Then send Hermione.

HELEN:
An unmarried girl cannot go alone to the grave.

ELECTRA:
It is her duty. She owes it to my mother for caring for her.

(*Helen pauses and then calls into the palace.*)

HELEN:
Hermione. (HERMIONE, *a young girl, appears from the palace.*)
Do as I say. Take this libation and this hair and go to Clytemnestra's grave. Pour this honey mild and wine over

the grave and as you pour say these words;
"Your sister Helen, stopped by the fear of the Argives from coming to your grave sends you these tokens." Then implore her to have mercy on my husband and me and on her poor children whom Apollo has destroyed.
Hurry and come back quickly.

(Exit Hermione with offerings. Helen goes into the palace.)

ELECTRA: *(Bitterly.)*
Did you see how she cut only the tips of her curls for her offering?

(ELECTRA'S *friends enter playing mournful music.)*

ELECTRA:
Walk softly friends. Your music, keep it low.

CHORUS:
He lies so still.

(ORESTES *suddenly stirs and wakes.)*

ORESTES:
Sweet wizard sleep. How I needed you.

ELECTRA:
How happy it made me to see you sleep at last.
Let me raise your head.

ORESTES:
Yes, please help me up.

ELECTRA:
Let me brush this poor matted hair.

ORESTES:
The fever makes me weary.

ELECTRA:
My brother lie back down and do not move.

(He lies down while she brushes his hair.)

ELECTRA:
Now listen. Listen Orestes. Our uncle Menelaus is here in Argos. His fleet lies at anchor at Nauplia.

ORESTES:
What? Is it true?
Then our darkness has a dawn.
Our father did so much for him.
He will help us.

ELECTRA:
There is more.
He has brought Helen home from Troy.

ORESTES:
Then he has brought sorrow home.

(Suddenly ORESTES *starts up wild eyed and screaming.)*

ELECTRA:
Orestes.

ORESTES:
Take the snakes away.
Take the snakes with gorgon eyes away.

ELECTRA:
Orestes there are no snakes.

ORESTES:
They want to kill me.

ELECTRA:
There are no snakes.

ORESTES:
Let me go. Aseme. I know you, you're one of the Furies too.
You're holding me down to hurl me into hell.

Oh my poor sister, how wrong it is that my madness
should hurt you so.
I think now if I had asked my dead father should I kill
our mother he would have begged me, gone down on his
knees and begged me not to take her life.
What had we to gain by murdering her?
Her death could never bring him back to life
and I, by killing her, have to suffer as I suffer now.
It is hopeless.
But do not cry. And sometimes when you see me mad from
desolation, comfort me and I in turn, when you despair,
will comfort you.
Our love is all we have.
Now go inside.
And rest.
If you fall ill then I will die. You are my only help.
My only hope.

ELECTRA:
I could never leave you Orestes. You are my hope too.
What am I without you?
A woman brotherless, fatherless, alone. *(She kisses him.)*
Rest if you can. *(She exits with bowl upper stage center.)*

CHORUS:
Eumenides, women of darkness,
avengers of murder,
we implore you—
release this boy,
from his madness

Happiness is brief.
It will not stay.
God batters at its sails,
sorrow strikes,
and happiness goes down,
and glory sinks.

Hail to the king who led a thousand ships to Troy.

MENELAUS:
Home at last. How happy I am to see this house once
more—
But also sad for never have I seen a house more hedged
about by suffering than this. Oh gods, is this some corpse I
see?

ORESTES:
It is I Uncle, your nephew.
I fall on my knees before you Menelaus.
and beg you to rescue us from death, you
who have led a thousand ships to Troy.

MENELAUS:
That stare in your eyes. When did this madness start?

ORESTES:
The day we built my mother's tomb. It came on me as I stood at the pyre.

MENELAUS:
That you should suffer is hardly strange. In Nauplia the sailors told me of the murder of Clytemnestra.

ORESTES:
It was Apollo who commanded my mother's murder.

MENELAUS:
A callous, unjust and immoral order.

ORESTES:
We obey the gods, whoever they may be.

MENELAUS:
How do you stand in the city?

ORESTES:
So hated and despised am I that not one person in Argos will speak to me. The city is voting on our sentence today.

MENELAUS:
Will they let you keep your father's sceptre?

ORESTES:
They do not want me to live.

MENELAUS:
What is the punishment — banishment or death?

ORESTES:
Death by stoning.

MENELAUS:
You must try to escape.

ORESTES:
Argos is surrounded by soldiers.
And that is why I turn to you, my father's brother.
You are our only hope.
Menelaus, we are desperate.
You have arrived in Argos prosperous and in your moment
of glory: I implore you to help us.

CHORUS:
Menelaus: Tyndareus of Sparta is on his way here.

ORESTES:
O gods.
What can I do?
Of all the men on this earth that I dread to meet it is my
grandfather Tyndareus who loved me more than his own
sons Castor and Polydeuces and who I loved as much as my
own father.
Where can I hide from my grandfather's eyes?

(*Enter* TYNDAREUS *gaunt in his seventies dressed in
mourning black. He too has attendants.*)

TYNDAREUS: (*To women.*)
Where can I find my daughter Helen's husband, Menelaus?

I was pouring libations on my daughter's grave when I heard the news of his arrival home at Nauplia after these long years.

MENELAUS: *(Seeing him.)*
Tyndareus!

TYNDAREUS:
Menelaus my son!

(He stops abruptly as he sees ORESTES.*)*

TYNDAREUS: *(Staring at Orestes.)*
o fon yas dis kor iz mo
o fon yas dis kor iz mo
o fon yas dis kor iz mo
o fon yas dis kor iz mo

MENELAUS:
Do not Tyndareus. Orestes is my brother's son.
And I loved my brother.

TYNDAREUS:
This murderer. *(Pause.)* As a boy I held him in my arms.

MENELAUS:
He is my brother's son in trouble.

TYNDAREUS:
Foreigners, I see, have taught you their ways.

MENELAUS:
It is a Greek custom, I think, to honor your kin.

TYNDAREUS:

But not to put yourself above the laws.
Not once did Orestes weigh the justice of his cause or seek our courts.
When his father died he should have made Clytemnestra pay by legal action not murder.
Now if anything the evil he has done has surpassed her crime.
If a wife murders her husband and her son then kills her then his son must have his murder.
Then this chain of murder can never end since the last to kill is doomed to a permanent sentence of death by revenge.
Our ancestors banned murderers from sight forbidding them to speak or meet with anyone: and by this they purge their guilt by banishment not death and by so they stop the cycle of revenge.
There I take my stand, attacking with all my heart,
the brutal spirit of murder that is corrupting
our cities and destroying this country.
You heard me Orestes; brutal.

One thing I know.
These fits of madness are what you pay for murder.
Heaven itself has made you mad. *(He starts to leave.)*

ORESTES:

Grandfather, please listen.
You who held me in your arms when I was a boy.
Listen.
I had every right to kill Clytemnestra.
She betrayed my father.
And I hated her.
She exiled my sister and me.
I had every right to kill her.

TYNDAREUS:
I came from Sparta to lay flowers on your
mother's grave but now by god I have a stronger motive:
your death.
I will go to the Argives myself and hound them until they
stone your sister and you. Yes, your sister.
It was Electra with her malice, telling you of her dreams of
Agamemnon's ghost and his cries from the grave that
incited you against your mother. *(Turning from* ORESTES.)
I warn you Menelaus do not oppose the gods by rescuing
Orestes and Electra.
(He exits. ORESTES *starts after him but is stopped by*
        MENELAUS.)

ORESTES: *(Falls at* MENELAUS' *feet.)*
Uncle, in honor of my dead father in his grave help us.

CHORUS:
Save them Menelaus.

MENELAUS:
Orestes I know we are joined by a common bond of blood
and I am honor bound to come to your defense against your
enemies.
I only wish I could. But I have arrived in Argos weakened.
My allies have dwindled away and I myself am exhausted
from this terrible ordeal.
We are weak and therefore our weapons must be diplomacy.
This is my plan.
I will go to the Argives and try to calm their fury and hope it
will burn itself out.
We have no other choice.
Be patient. The winds may shift. *(*MENELAUS *exits.)*

ORESTES:

You traitor! What have you ever done but fight a war to bring your wife back home? So now you turn your back and desert me.

This is the end.

This is the last of the house of Agamemnon.

My poor father deserted by his kin.

And now my last hope from death is lost . . . Menelaus.

(Enter PYLADES.*)*

PYLADES:

I seem to have come none too soon Orestes.

As I was coming through the town I saw the Argives meeting and heard them discussing a plan to execute Electra and you.

ORESTES:
We are ruined.

PYLADES:
As matters stand now our deaths are certain.

ORESTES:
Our?

PYLADES:
You, Electra, and I are one.

ORESTES:
They vote on the sentence today.

PYLADES:
Take Electra and try to escape.

ORESTES:
Sentries are patrolling the streets.
We are surrounded like a city under siege.

PYLADES:
I have suffered too.

ORESTES:
Something else has happened?

PYLADES:
My father has banished me from Phocis.

ORESTES:
Heaven help us. *(Silence.)*

What am I supposed to do? Die without saying a word in
my own defense?

PYLADES:
There is nothing to gain from staying here but if you go to
the meeting then something might be gained. But you may
be killed.

ORESTES:
But I must go. *(Pause.)*

My madness. What if I have an attack?
Madmen are hard to handle.

PYLADES:
I will manage.

ORESTES:
But if my madness strikes you too?

PYLADES:
I am not afraid.

ORESTES:
Then take me first to my father's grave.
I want to pray and implore his help.

PYLADES:
Good.

ORESTES:
But Pylades, don't let me see my mother's grave.

PYLADES:
I will not.
We must go now.
Here lean on me.
Let the people jeer.
I'll lead you through the city unashamed.
What is friendship worth unless I prove it in this time of trouble.

(They exit.)

CHORUS:
Glory decays, and
greatness goes
from the happy house of Atreus.
Beneath the proud facade
the long stain spread

as the curse of blood began—
strife for a golden ram,
slaughter of little princes,
a table laid with horror,
a feast of murdered sons.
And still corruption swelled,
murder displacing murder,
to reach at last
the living heirs of Atreus.

What terror can compare with us?

Hands of a son,
Stained with his mother's blood.

(ELECTRA *appears from the palace and is frightened to find*
ORESTES *gone.*)

ELECTRA: *(To women.)*
Where is Orestes? Has his madness come again?

CHORUS:
No Electra. He went to the Argive meeting to speak in his
own defense.

ELECTRA:
But why? Who persuaded him?

CHORUS:
Pylades.

(Enter messenger.)

MESSENGER:
Princess Electra.
I bring you sad news.

ELECTRA: *(Pause.)*
Our sentence is death.

MESSENGER:
Yes. The Argives voted that you and your brother must die
today.

ELECTRA:
And how are we to die my brother and I?

MESSENGER:
Poor Orestes was just able to persuade them not to stone
you both to death by promising that you and he would kill
yourselves this day.
Pylades is bringing him home.
So bring out the sword for you must leave this light.
Apollo has destroyed you both.

ELECTRA: *(Trembling.)*
Down and down my house.
Pelops line is ended.
Down and down
Greatness has gone from the house of Atreus
Ending with this curse on my brother and me.
i thei namas vo i thi sun

(Enter ORESTES *supported by* PYLADES. ELECTRA *bursts
into tears at the sight of him.)*

ELECTRA:
Orestimu Orestimu

(ORESTES *kissing her.*)

ORESTES:
No more Electra.
What shame on earth can touch me anymore?
O my sister, this last sweet embrace is all
we shall ever know of love and marriage.
Our time has come.
We must choose the sword or the rope.

ELECTRA:
Kill me yourself Orestes.

ORESTES:
I cannot my sister.

ELECTRA:
If only one sword could kill us both. If we could only share
one coffin together.

ORESTES:
No . . . we must die as we were born . . . well . . . as the
children of Agamemnon.
I shall show Argos of what blood I come by
falling on my sword and you must follow and die bravely.
Pylades lay us out and make us both one grave beside my
father's tomb.

PYLADES:
My friend how could you think I would want to live if you
were dead?

ORESTES:
Pylades.
You have your country, your father's house and wealth.
Marry and have heirs. The bonds which bound us once are
broken now. Goodbye my only friend.

PYLADES:
I murdered with you. I helped plan the crime for which you
suffer and now I should die with you and Electra.
It is my duty. *(Pause.)*

Wait! But since we have to die, is there not some way to
make Menelaus suffer. He did not one thing to help his
brother's children.

ORESTES:
How could he be avenged?

PYLADES:
Listen: we will avenge him by murdering Helen.

ORESTES:
There is no way we could do this.

PYLADES:
Yes there is. We'll go inside the palace pretending that we
are about to kill ourselves.

ORESTES:
And then?

PYLADES:
We will weep and tell her how much we suffer.
Then she will pretend to weep.

We'll carry the swords hidden in our robes and while she pretends this grief we'll lock her slaves in different rooms.

ORESTES:
Then death to Helen.

PYLADES:
Not only do we avenge her for ourselves, but we avenge her in the name of all Hellas, whose fathers and sons she murdered.
There will be celebrations in Argos.
Men will bless our heads and sing songs of glory to us for doing away with her.
Should we fail we'll burn this house around us as we die.
Orestes you shall not be cheated of honor.

(ELECTRA, *who has been sitting, joins in.*)

ELECTRA:
Listen Orestes: you too Pylades. Do you remember Helen's daughter, Hermione?

ORESTES:
The little girl our mother took care of?

ELECTRA:
Yes. Well she has now gone to Clytemnestra's grave to pour libations there.

ORESTES:
What has this to do with our escape?

ELECTRA:
When she comes back we will seize her.

ORESTES:
How will that help us?

ELECTRA:
We must have a plan. Once Helen is dead Menelaus may
attempt to capture one of us. And if he tries, we will set our
sword at Hermione's throat and warn him, we will kill her.
If then seeing Helen lying in a pool of blood, he decides he
wants his daughter's life, and agrees to spare us, we will let
Hermione go. But if he tries to kill one of us in a mad rage
then we will slit her throat.
He is a coward as we have seen. I believe he will not fight.
And there you have my plan for making our escape.

ORESTES:
I like this plan.
How soon do you think Hermione will return?

ELECTRA:
Any moment now.

ORESTES:
Then Electra you stay here and wait for her return. Make
certain that no one and no friend of her father's enters the
palace. But if someone does beat your fist on the door and
raise the cry. But let us know. Pylades and I will go inside
now to Helen. Have your sword ready.

*(He raises his arms in prayer and invokes the ghost of
Agamemnon.)*

ORESTES:
O my father, ghost who walks the black house of Atreus,
your son Orestes calls upon your help in his hour of need.

It is for you father I suffer.
For you I was condemned to death unfairly.
And your own brother has betrayed me though what I did
was right. Come father, help me to capture Helen.
Help me kill her.
O Father help us now.

ELECTRA:
O father if you can hear our prayers beneath the earth know
that we die for you.

PYLADES:
O Agamemnon kinsman of my father.
Hear my prayers.
Save your children.

ORESTES:
I murdered my mother.

PYLADES:
I held the sword that killed.

ELECTRA:
I was their spirit.
I made them brave.

ORESTES:
I offer my tears to you.

ELECTRA:
And I my grief.

PYLADES:
Enough. If prayers can penetrate this earth he hears.

We must go about this business now.
Three friends together. One common cause. Together we
shall live or die.

ELECTRA:
Women of Argos, a word with you please.

CHORUS:
What is it Princess Electra?

ELECTRA:
I want half of you to watch the road and the rest will stand
guard here.

(Women divide.)

CHORUS:
I'll watch the road to the east.

And I'll watch here on the westward side.

All's well here. Not an Argive in sight.

Nor here either. Not a soldier in sight.

ELECTRA:
Then wait. *(She calls inside the palace to* ORESTES *and*
PYLADES.*)*

Why are you so quiet?
They don't answer. Not a sound. O Zeus. Has her beauty
blinded them too?

(Suddenly from within the palace.)

HELEN:
Help me Argos.
They're murdering me.
They're murdering me.

ELECTRA:
O Zeus send us strength.
Help us now.

HELEN:
Help me I'm dying . . .
vo i thia pe the no

ELECTRA:
Run the traitoress through.
Kill the whore who killed so many brave men.

CHORUS:
Electra we hear the sound of footsteps. Someone is coming.

ELECTRA:
It must be Hermione. Yes it is Hermione herself.
Quiet, not a sound. Appear natural as though nothing has
happened here. *(Enter* HERMIONE.*)*

Hermione have you returned from Clytemnestra's grave
and did you circle it with flowers and pour libations?

HERMIONE:
Yes I paid her the dues of the dead. *(Pause.)*
But what has happened here? I thought I heard a scream in
the distance.

ELECTRA:
A scream?

HERMIONE:
What has happened?

ELECTRA:
Orestes and I have been sentenced to death.

HERMIONE:
Zeus, Zeus.

ELECTRA:
And he went and fell at Helen's knees.

HERMIONE:
I don't understand.

ELECTRA:
Orestes went to implore Helen to save our lives.

HERMIONE:
Then that was the cry I heard?

ELECTRA:
Yes and if you love us go now, fall at your mother's feet and
beg her.
Implore her to intercede with Menelaus on our behalf.
You are our very last hope.

HERMIONE:
Oh yes. I will go now. If it lies in my power you are saved.

(HERMIONE *enters the palace.*)

Ach Mi ter a mu

ORESTES: *(From inside the palace.)*
Silence Hermione. You are here to save us.

ELECTRA:
Seize her and stop her screaming. Let Menelaus learn what
it is to fight with men, not cowards from Troy. Make him
suffer for his indifference to us.

*(ELECTRA enters the palace closing the doors behind her.
From inside are cries and muffled screams.)*

CHORUS:
Quick raise a shout, a cry to drown the sound of murder in
the palace before the Argives hear.

Be still. Be still.
It is a Trojan slave. He will tell us what has happened. Be still.

*(A TROJAN SLAVE incoherent from terror bursts from the
palace.)*

TROJAN SLAVE:
Trojan scared and run,
clamber over the roof.
O
Ilium,
Ilium Troy
hear the dirge I cry ai ai.
Out of hiding
Out of purple cloaks
they drew their swords and eyes of them. O going round to
see if danger anywhere and then they came.

They were yes shouting and screaming
die die die for traitor husband coward who
betrayed his brother's son
who left him to die in Argos.
Lady Helen screamed white arms flailing
flailing beating bosom beating breast
hair she tore in sandals leaped to run
but after after came Orestes.
Caught her O winding fingers in her hair
and neck forced back
down down
against her shoulder and lifted
the sword to strike.

CHORUS:
Where were the servants?

TROJAN SLAVE:
We batter doors with iron bars break down panels.
Then run some with stones.
Pylades came on brave Hectorlike or Ajax.
Steel on steel together meet but soon we see
Trojan men, ai ai one run dead
wounding this and begging that
near the dirge I cry ai ai
falling some dying others
staggering is one with wounds.
And then Hermione came in as mother Helen sank to die.
O Earth O Night.
What then happen I do not know.

CHORUS:
Now retribution follows sin.
Through the fated house more winds blow.

And through the rooms round the stone cornice
Ring out new death cries.
Grief has come down once more
On the house of Atreus.

(Enter MENELAUS *with armed men.)*

MENELAUS:
I have heard this tale of brutal and mad crimes committed
by Electra and Orestes.
Men break down the door so that I can rescue my dear
daughter from these murderers and bring out Helen's body.
In revenge for her I shall put them to death.

(Suddenly from the roof comes billowing smoke.)

CHORUS:
Look on the roof of the palace. *(Slowly smoke rises. They
    watch.)*

They are burning the ancestral house.

MENELAUS:
Madness has consumed them.

(The door opens; behind it ORESTES *is holding a knife to*
    HERMIONE'S *throat.)*

MENELAUS:
mi och i tin(z) ko ri mo
Why are you holding my daughter?
Wasn't it enough that you murdered her mother?

ORESTES:
And now I will kill your daughter.

MENELAUS:
But why?

ORESTES:
You betrayed us Menelaus.

MENELAUS:
Wasn't Clytemnestra's death enough?

ORESTES:
Helen and Clytemnestra were whores.

MENELAUS:
But Hermione?

ORESTES:
Hermione's death will be to avenge my father.
And now we'll burn this doomed palace.

MENELAUS:
Burn the house of Atreus?

ORESTES:
To keep it from you Menelaus. But first the sword at
Hermione's throat.

(*Among the armed men and women there is great commotion and cries in Greek: ti ka non ti ji ne te.*)

MENELAUS:
Could you kill my child?

What is it that you want?

(Cries in Greek: prepi na skoto thun.)

ORESTES:
Persuade the people.

MENELAUS:
Persuade them of what?

ORESTES:
To let us live traitor.

MENELAUS:
Or you kill my child?

ORESTES:
Yes.

MENELAUS:
Then I am trapped.

ORESTES:
Yes trapped by your own mercilessness.
Electra burn the parapet
Pylades set the roof to blazes.

MENELAUS:
Vo i thi a
Strati ote tu argo
Vo i thia

(Chaos ensues. Suddenly APOLLO *appears in the palace doorway.)*

APOLLO:

Cease Menelaus. It is I Pheobus Apollo.

Helen is here with me. Orestes did not kill her.

Helen, being born of Zeus, could not die

and now will sit enthroned forever, a star for sailors.

It is Orestes' destiny to leave Argos and journey to the city of Athena and give justice for his mother's murder. The gods on the hill of Ares shall be his judges and acquit him in a sacred verdict.

Then Orestes will marry Hermione.

Electra shall marry Pylades as promised.

Happiness awaits him.

Menelaus will be king in Sparta and I shall give Argos to Orestes . . . for it was I who commanded his mother's murder. I compelled him to kill.

ORESTES:

Hail Apollo for your oracles. And yet sometimes when I heard you speak to me it seemed the whispers of a monster. But all is well now and I obey. See I release Hermione and we shall marry if her father gives his blessing.

MENELAUS:

I envy your happiness with the gods. Orestes I betroth Hermione to you as Apollo commands.

APOLLO: *(Dismissing them.)*

Go and honor peace now. Helen I now lead to the halls of Zeus among the blazing stars, there with Hera she shall sit a goddess forever and reign the seas, a light to sailors.

(The palace door closes.)

CURTAIN

Adrienne
KENNEDY

Adrienne Kennedy began to write and have her plays
produced in the 1960s. She has been commissioned to
write plays for the Public Theater, Jerome Robbins, The
Royal Court, and Julliard. Kennedy has been a visiting lec-
turer at many universities, including New York University,
the University of California at Berkeley, and Harvard. Her
plays are part of college curricula in the United States,
Europe, and Africa. Kennedy is the recipient of an award
in literature from the American Academy of Arts and
Letters, a Lila Wallace–Reader's Digest Fund Writers'
Award, the Pierre LeComte duNouy Foundation Award,
and three Obies. Kennedy's autobiography, *People Who
Led to My Plays*, was published by Knopf in 1987 and is
currently available in paperback from Theatre
Communications Group.